Hunting Rutting Bucks

OUTDOORSMAN'S EDGE®

Hunting Rutting Bucks

SECRETS FOR TAGGING THE BIGGEST BUCK OF YOUR LIFE!

John Trout, Jr.

Acknowledgments

I had always hoped to do a book about hunting rutting whitetail bucks. Because there is so much more to the rut than bucks chasing does, I wanted the book to go deeply into each phase—pre-rut, primary rut and post-rut. I thank Kate and Peter Fiduccia of Woods N' Water, Inc. for making it all happen.

On more than one occasion in this book, I discuss anecdotes. Some of these mention my son John. I thank him for the time we have shared outdoors, and for the unforgettable stories he has contributed. It was so enjoyable writing these anecdotes; the memories will last forever. I look forward to those that are yet to come.

My wife, Vikki, has always been there for me. Her support for this book, her hand at proof-reading, and her time helping with photography cannot go unmentioned. But more than anything, I thank her for sharing time with me in the deer-hunting woods. What a blessing it has been.

Hunting mature whitetail bucks has never been and never will be easy. However, my good friend Tim Hillsmeyer has made the job a little less painful, helping me become a wiser and better hunter. I thank him for his friendship and for the knowledge he has shared over the years. Between the covers of this book, he now shares some of that knowledge with you.

Hunting is truly a wonderful experience, but companionship makes it better.

I thank Dad, and so many other friends who have made my time in the outdoors so enjoyable. I thank them, too, for being so willing to stop and pose for photographs at a moment's notice.

Finally, I thank my God for supporting me, for the hunting opportunities. He has given me the perfect creations and beautiful landscapes I have viewed. It is not the first time I have said this, and it won't be the last.

Dedication

This book is dedicated to Tim, whose friendship and knowledge has contributed to my passionate pursuit of trophy whitetails.

Front cover image: John Trout, Jr.
Back cover images: John Trout, Jr.
All images by author unless noted otherwise.

Published by: Woods N' Water, Inc.
Peter and Kate Fiduccia
P.O. Box 550
Florida, NY 10921

Printed in the United States of America
10 9 8 7 6 5 4 3 2 1
ISBN: 0-9722804-6-4

TABLE OF CONTENTS

Introduction

For just a moment, stop and think about the "rut." You probably visualize a huge buck on the move in pursuit of a hot doe. Yep, that's a good description and a fair judgment. But as the old saying goes, "That's not all folks."

Let me remind you of one important fact: More often than not, we tag trophy bucks because they did something wrong—not because we did something right. With that out of the way, I can proceed and tell you how this book can help you to reverse that fact.

The rut consists of hundreds of factors that lead up to the moment of breeding. These aspects occur in three cycles, and they all tie together, like a complete and perfect puzzle. It begins during pre-rut, slowly progresses into the primary rut, and tapers off during the post-rut. Any deer hunter with bow or gun who understands these factors, and knows when in the cycle a given factor will occur, is conceivably a major step closer to tagging a trophy whitetail buck.

If there's one misconception about the rut, it has to be that most individuals consider it to be only a period of a few days when all bucks are vulnerable and about to commit the biggest mistake of their lives. For the remainder of this book, we'll pitch that theory right out the door. As you will see in the pages that follow, the rut lasts for months. Sometimes it's hot. Sometimes it's not. It can be dead one hour and come to life the next. However, the rut is always an opportunity for deer hunters, and that's what this book is about. It provides an array of advanced tactics for each stage of the rut—from the onset of the first day to the final moments of the last.

As a collector of vintage hunting magazines, I've had many chances to read lots of old publications. If, like me, you've ever enjoyed a glance through those published before the 1950s, you probably noticed that deer-hunting articles focused on the basics—stalking or waiting in ambush along a trail between a food source and a bedding area. Seeing the term "rut" was as rare as finding a walnut hanging on an oak tree.

Today's deer-hunting stories are far different and many have a distinct focus on the rut. There have been several books written about bucks in rut, not to mention countless magazine articles. However, even the rut-topic pieces of today tend to focus on one phase in particular, making it doubly difficult to understand the rut in its entirety.

I've always looked at the rut as a long continuation of habits. Consider a few of my magazine articles. I recall one titled "The Pre-Rut Frenzy," which told why bucks are often vulnerable several weeks before the primary rut. Then there was one called "Hot Scrapes or Rub Lines" that discussed the best of those to hunt when the breeding had begun. Moreover, I can't forget one of my post-rut pieces called "Late-Season Madness," which gave the details of ambushing bucks as they busily enjoyed the second rut. Each ranged from 2,000 to 2,500 words, but word count was the only thing these rut-hunting stories had in common. They never discussed the same tactics.

In this book, you'll find proven tactics for pursuing bucks in each phase of the rut, beginning to end, with an emphasis on trophy whitetail bucks. Certainly, what is a trophy buck in the eyes of one person might be different in the eyes of another. Thus, when I say "trophy" I mean "mature." And although mature bucks practice rutting habits similar to those of younger bucks, there are differences, as you'll soon read about. You're likely to be amazed by what you discover.

This book leans toward the advanced stages of pursuing mature bucks. It will get you off overused master trails and into those areas where perseverance can lead you to a big buck.

You'll read about both bow and gun hunting techniques. Some tactics will apply to one or the other. Some strategies will apply to both methods. There are also plenty of anecdotes, since I've always believed one of the best ways to perceive a certain point is to share someone else's firsthand experience.

Although I did not include detailed chapters devoted exclusively to bow- or gun-hunting tactics, you'll find I get descriptive about each.

For instance, I have been an avid archery hunter ever since I started pursuing whitetails more than forty years ago. For me, hunting always begins on the first day of the early archery season and continues until the last day of the late-archery season, if I carry an unfilled tag. Even if I do not have a tag, I'm usually setting up stands and continuing to be of help to someone. Thus, my deer hunting is seldom interrupted by schedules outside of the woods.

Between the archery seasons, I don't miss an opportunity to hunt with gun, be it during the regular firearm season or the special blackpowder season. You get the point. I love the outdoors and relish every hunting occasion. This multitude of experiences has given me an insight on the rut, and made it possible for me to shoot several huge bucks.

Now that you know I hunt with both bow and gun and whenever opportunity allows, I will tell you that even when I hunt with a firearm, I always think like a bowhunter. It has allowed me to get close to big rutting bucks, and it has certainly been a plus for filling tags.

Another point I should make is that certain dates in the rut won't be discussed. The primary-rut period, for example, might occur around November 10 where I reside but not until about December 30 in your area. Thus, it wouldn't make much sense to provide a certain date as the best time to perform any given tactic. The primary rut is decided by lots of factors including latitude, which is why the primary rut in Alabama is considerably later than the same phase in Minnesota.

Speaking of primary rut, I originally considered calling the second phase "peak-rut." My publisher and seasoned deer hunting veteran, Peter Fiduccia, rightfully suggested I use the term "primary rut," and rightfully so. The primary rut lasts for a period of a few days, while the peak is actually a much shorter episode, limited to 24 hours at most. When discussing the primary rut in this book, you'll see the mention of peak only as it is used to pinpoint the hottest day of the season.

The rut-hunting tactics herein are based upon "smart" deer. In other words, I have hunted all my life in areas where hunting pressure has always existed. Sometimes it has been public land, sometimes private. Sometimes one area gets more pressure than others. However, never have I hunted behind a fence, nor has anyone else associated with this book. So the strategies I discuss cannot be relied upon if you are accustomed to fence hunts.

Before going on, let me say a little more about fenced hunt operations. They have long been a way for some landowners to make money, and it is true that the size of an operation matters. The bigger the area, the more wary whitetails become, which is why it doesn't bother some folks to hunt behind a fence. However, the amount of acreage does not eliminate certain facts: Fenced operations control their own harvests. No wild deer can come in or out. Supplemental feeding is a factor. Genetics are purchased, some for breeding purposes and some for being shot "Johnny-on-the-spot." Even on large amounts of acreage, many deer in the enclosure are bottle-fed deer and raised by humans. Enough said. It's your business if you hunt behind a fence and I'm not necessarily passing judgment. But that is why I say the advanced rut-hunting tactics in this book apply only to "smart" deer.

The book is divided into three sections, one on each phase of the rut—pre-rut, primary and post-rut—and each section contains several chapters. The book begins at the moment the velvet comes off the antlers and ends when the antlers are shed.

You'll find the pre-rut section to a bit longer than the others, simply because this period offers the best opportunities to pattern and kill a mature buck.

You'll read about early-autumn rubs and discover which ones offer the best hunting opportunities. There's a chapter about the methods for deciphering the types of trails you come across, and for determining whether to hunt rubs or scrapes. You'll also read about tracking a wounded buck during primary rut, and how it compares to tracking one in the pre-rut or post-rut periods.

Any hunter who kills big bucks consistently has not been privileged enough to always be in the right place at the right time. Individuals that have done so have mastered the rut in its entirety. That's what this book is all about. In reading it cover-to-cover, and allowing the photos to speak for themselves, you'll master the rutting tricks-of-the-trade, and learn more about the habits of the whitetail than you ever dreamed possible.

–John Trout, Jr.

SECTION ONE
The Pre-Rut

1
Anatomy of the Pre-Rut

It's late summer, the time of year when whitetail bucks commonly hang together, sometimes grooming each other and removing insects. They share the same bedding areas, trails and food sources. They have no quarrels to speak of. Their antlers are covered in velvet, necks remain thin and the breeding is months away. Amazingly, within days it will all change. While many deer hunters are occupied with outside projects and not yet thinking about the deer woods, the velvet on antlers will come off, testicles will swell and testosterone will rise. The pre-rut period has begun!

A buck's antlers start growing the moment he sheds them in winter or early spring, although they won't be visible for several weeks. The antlers will grow hour by hour, reaching maximum size by the middle of summer, when bucks' testosterone is at its lowest level. That's not to say a buck won't breed if opportunity allows.

I have been fortunate to study several pen-raised whitetails over the years. One old doe named Julie gave birth to fawns each summer from the time she was two-years-old until she turned eight. She has had no more fawns since after her eighth birthday, even though she remains quite healthy and her teeth still get the job done on the high-protein diet she is fed. Despite not impregnating, though, she comes into estrous in late November or early December each year and continues to breed. Sis (don't ask how he got that name), a seven-year-old buck in the same pen, always

By midsummer the antlers harden and a buck's testosterone level begins to rise.

A captive doe named Julie is shown here with the last two fawns she had at age eight. Now eleven years old, she still breeds from November through March, although she never becomes impregnated.

breeds her, and breeds her and breeds her. In fact, Julie and Sis breed monthly up until April.

Sis typically loses his antlers in February. Thus, even though his testosterone is at its lowest, he won't pass up a golden opportunity. I should add, he breeds other does and all of them give birth to fawns each year, so clearly Julie's lack of fawns is not due to any problem with Sis. For all this Sis is grateful, even though he's worn out and down to skin-and-bones when the breeding finally ends.

By the way, at the time of this writing, Julie is eleven-years-old and still breeding at least five months out of the year like she always has, with twenty-four to twenty-eight days between her breeding episodes. Research has shown that some does have bred six times without impregnating. Wouldn't you like to have one like that running around in your hunting area?

When you stop and think about it, it's good news that the old doe doesn't impregnate when bred in spring—one of nature's marvels. It makes certain that fawns will be born when they have the best chance of surviving. Consider that a doe will carry a fawn more than two hundred days. Cold weather and scarcity of food would make it difficult on both the fawn and doe if she gave birth in November.

It is the long daylight hours of summer that cause a buck's hormones to increase and testicles to grow–the first progressive stage of the pre-rut period. This is when sperm first appear in his semen and blood stops circulating in the velvet covering of his antlers.

Some hunters have gotten the idea that velvet comes off the antlers because of rubbing, but the skin is actually ready to come off soon after the bone hardens.

Once the blood no longer flows through, the velvet decays, shreds and begins to separate from the antlers. Portions might hang by threads, often prompting a buck to scrape his antlers against a bush, tree, or the ground in an attempt to rid the nuisance. Bucks make it a point not to leave even one small piece of the velvet. When the velvet is first removed, the antlers might have a reddish color, which is actually a blood stain. Some claim the entire velvet-shedding process can take up to thirty-six hours, although I have never seen it last more than twenty-four. In every case,

I have observed a buck one day, only to see his velvet gone the next.

The removal of the velvet, and the thrashing of antlers against objects to remove it, seem to spark the buck's desire to rub trees, an act of frustration and, actually, another sexual stage of the pre-rut. Bucks love to get real nasty, breaking and destroying anything within their power. Locating and hunting these early-autumn rubs are often beneficial, as you'll read later in this pre-rut section. Keep in mind, once a buck starts rubbing in the pre-rut season, he may rub several trees daily.

The pre-rut phase begins the moment bucks begin shedding their velvet. The velvet is usually removed within twenty-four hours.

It's also true that some bucks, particularly young ones, will begin sparring within days of removing the velvet. Sparring builds up neck muscles for future battles and establishes who's king-of-the-hill. Some young bucks probably spar for entertainment. Regardless of why bucks spar, it is the reason that rattling often lures them in during the pre-rut period.

I've spent hours photographing wild turkeys and have recorded numerous pecking order fights among the toms when breeding occurs, but pecking order events among whitetails are different. The only ones I've seen had nothing to do with the rut. In areas where numerous mature bucks exist, a hierarchy is usually established before the breeding begins, usually during the early portion of the pre-rut. This can change in late pre-rut, or during primary rut. When one buck overlaps another's territory, knock-down, drag-out fights can occur. During pre-rut, most mature bucks will not challenge each other, unless there's a breeding doe around.

Sparring begins almost the moment velvet is removed and intensifies as autumn progresses. It is one of the first noticeable gestures behaviors of the pre-rut phase, even though mature bucks do very little sparring, if any sparring.

Note the distinction between fights and spars. Sparring is quite friendly and more of a practice amongst young bucks than mature ones. When they spar, bucks poke antlers without much force and shove at each other with little energy. When bucks actually fight, body size is just as much a factor as antler size, and the energy behind the pushing, antlers against antlers, often decides the winner.

Some buck fights never get started during the pre-rut period only because one buck simply intimidated another by slicking back his ears against his neck. His hair rises like he just stuck his hoof in an electrical socket, and the aggressive gestures often scare away an opponent.

Bachelor groups are common in both late summer and even early autumn after the velvet has shed. Does usually avoid bucks, but it doesn't really matter since the bucks don't really want to hang out with the does. What's crucial for hunters to know is that mature bucks in pre-rut seem to have their own areas away from other bucks. They tend to form their own groups or, more often, they hang out alone. It's uncommon to see a three- or four-year-old buck hanging out with two or three others just past their first birthday. The bachelor groups typically fall apart before or within days of the velvet shedding.

Scraping in the pre-rut period is common. Bucks often begin scraping the ground shortly after removing the velvet, although some deer have been noted scraping one month before the velvet came off. Pre-rut scrapes typically show up along fringes, but bucks seldom visit them regularly. Scrapes that include "licking branches" and applications of glandular substances are usually the most important. These usually start showing up about one week before the breeding begins, and I've found that the more bucks there are in a given area, the more pre-rut scraping occurs.

However, I have never enjoyed success hunting scrapes during pre-rut. Hunting scrapes is tough business anytime, but I believe early-season scrapes only cost you precious time. In other words, you will have the best chance of killing a mature buck during the pre-rut season if you concentrate on other tactics. (The primary rut is a different story, which you'll read about later.)

The difference of what happens in each of these rut phases is astronomical. Although we commonly see doe-chasing occur during the primary rut, it's far more typical of the pre-rut. A young buck will consistently "bird-dog," coming up behind a doe and rapidly approaching for a short distance of about thirty yards, stomping his feet hard against the ground, with his head low and his neck extended as far as it can go. Mature bucks seldom chase does in pre-rut, knowing the time is not right. They wait, and will even tolerate the younger bucks making total fools of themselves.

In late summer and even early autumn, mature bucks often hang together. This routine subsides shortly after the velvet is removed.

We know that decreasing sunlight affects the estrous cycle of the does just as it affects the testosterone rise in bucks. The difference, during pre-rut at least, is that does give no outward signals of the coming rut—at least none that researchers and hunters can see. Bucks rub antlers, make scrapes and get aggressive. Does don't pay any attention to scrapes, nor do anything aggressively with their heads and glands, and they don't care about other does of the same age group nearby. Make no mistake, though, the pre-rut phase is working on them, and the bucks know it, probably through the scent of the does' gland secretions and urine .

So how long does the pre-rut last? Of the three phases—pre-rut, primary rut and post-rut—the pre-rut and post-rut periods offer the longest hunting opportunities. The primary rut is shorter—governed by the does' major but brief breeding cycle—

7

and typically lasts for about two weeks, including a peak-day. Thus, consider that one week before and one week after that peak day is the primary rut period. Every moment that follows the bucks' loss of velvet, up to one week before the primary rut, can be considered the pre-rut period. This could be just a few weeks or perhaps several.

Most bucks in a given area will shed their velvet during a two-week period, but not all bucks in the area lose their velvet the same day. I remember seeing one buck in the process of losing his on August 13—extremely early for the area I was in—and another buck in the same area with his velvet peeling off during the second week of September of the same year. Researchers have noted that older bucks often

lose their velvet before yearling bucks, primarily because of higher peaks in testosterone levels.

Consider, too, that breeding starts earlier in some areas than others because decreasing sunlight is not the only factor that controls buck and doe hormones, as once believed. For this reason, some bucks and does breed as early as September, while others breed in November and some breed in January.

The length of the pre-rut phase is dependant upon when the breeding begins. In some areas, the breeding begins as early as September, although in most regions it will begin some time between November and January.

There is no question in my mind that weather affects your chances of intercepting a pre-rut buck. During the breeding season, weather might not matter as much, but when the bugs are plentiful and Indian summer persists, it can hurt. I've most certainly had better luck some years than others, simply because of temperatures and an early arrival of the first frost. Nevertheless, don't think for a moment you can't kill a mature buck if it's ninety degrees and mosquitoes are buzzing. Many hunters have done so because they patterned a buck.

I've always said that anyone can kill a buck during the primary rut if they hunt hard. You only have to be a little lucky to end up in the right area at right moment. It takes little scouting to get lucky, and little knowledge of a rutting buck's habits to take advantage of an easy kill. Bucks make mistakes by moving consistently in search of does. Some folks hunt all their lives hoping to shoot a record-book deer,

Unlike bucks in the breeding season, when bucks often move through open areas at any hour of the day, bucks during the pre-rut seldom make those mistakes.

yet some individuals do it on opening day the first time they go hunting, but only because that hunt took place at the peak of the breeding period. That's not to say that any of us can shoot a mature buck every season during rut just by getting lucky, however. Section II of this book includes several chapters dedicated to tactics for killing big bucks during rut. I'm just saying that the primary rut is the easiest time to get the job done.

On the other hand, I believe hunters who have enjoyed successes in pre-rut have accomplished great feats. During pre-rut, bucks are not vulnerable and prone to making "dumb" mistakes. Whitetails have always been creatures of habit, but during pre-rut, they stick even closer to certain rules. They seldom move about four hours after dawn or four hours before dusk like they often do in primary rut. They seldom cover a mile or two overnight and wind up in a strange area, like they consistently do in primary rut. They seldom cross open fields in the middle of the day or bed down just anywhere they happen to be, like they often do in primary rut.

Nevertheless, a good hunter can cause bucks in pre-rut to make mistakes. As I just said, deer are creatures of habit in late summer and early autumn, and this sets the stage for patterning a buck during the pre-rut period. Figure out what he's eating and where he's bedding, get to understand his personality, and he could be yours. That's all easier said than accomplished, but some hunters have taken plenty of big whitetails during the pre-rut period because they patterned a buck accurately.

A limited home range makes it easier to pattern bucks in the pre-rut period, although the distance they roam will vary from area-to-area. Weather, predators, and hunting pressure play a key role. However, most of the time during primary rut a buck says goodbye to his home range and, as you know, many never make it back.

In pre-rut, a mature buck's home range might be only a hundred acres or up to a square mile. The latter is usually not the case in pre-rut. Either way, you can bet that when the breeding begins, a buck won't be spending much time at home.

In early autumn, most deer refuse to leave their home range. For example, a 1970 study indicated that one young buck fitted with a radio collar was chased out of his home range by dogs on several occasions. He always returned within a few hours. After so many chases, he finally set up a temporary home a long way off, only to return close to the home range on a couple of other occasions. The young buck spent the primary rut in an entirely new area.

Does typically have smaller home ranges than bucks. One five-year study in Texas showed that some does shared a home range of about 93 acres, two does had larger ranges of 502 acres, while another had a home range of 690 acres. The same study indicated the bucks had an average home range of 1,079 acres. Researchers noted, however, that the deer's home range decreased in spring and summer when bucks were growing antlers and does were with fawns. The does then kept their home ranges to twenty-four acres and, strangely, the bucks settled for thirteen.

Another interesting study occurred on Crab Orchard National Wildlife Refuge in Illinois. It showed that in 1962, only one percent of the deer observed early in the year on the refuge were killed elsewhere later that year, compared to seventeen percent in 1965. The researcher linked the difference to increasing population and human pressure.

As for mature bucks, I'm not so sure they get as far away from their home range as do young bucks. I'm speaking of the primary rut, of course. It's just that I have seen several big bucks in one area during the pre-rut, only to see them again in the primary rut close to where they were the first time. I sincerely believe that mature bucks become home-range conscious, seeming to prefer an area they know best as opposed to one they know nothing about. This is probably the exception to the rule, but I mention it just to let you know that if you don't get a certain buck in the pre-rut phase, you could get lucky and see him again in the same vicinity after the breeding begins.

We could assume that the more an area is left alone, the better the chance that those bucks in the area will remain there, at least through the pre-rut phase. Intense interruptions in a bedding area or some form of harassment along trails and in feeding areas may force a deer away long before the primary rut arrives. With these facts in mind, we should view it as a demonstration of how we can easily cause harm to the areas we hunt.

I know of some archery hunters who claim this is why they do not want to hunt before the primary rut arrives. They know that if their presence becomes known, it's all over but the shouting.

Although the stakes are high during the pre-rut period, the rewards are worth the effort. One goof is all it takes to let a home-range buck know he's being hunted. However, the pre-rut is one of the best times to pattern a mature deer.

I don't agree. First, I love hunting too much to limit myself to only the primary rut. Although I know how important it is to remain undetected during the pre-rut, I also realize that it's the prime time to pattern a buck and kill him. I look at it this way: You only need to sharpen your hunting skills to make sure you don't interrupt a buck's habits before killing him. And if you do screw up a big buck during the pre-rut, the game is not necessarily over.

From experience, I can tell you that big bucks won't always leave the country during the pre-rut just because they know you are hunting them. As mentioned previously, even the young buck was run out of his home range by dogs numerous times before he finally gave it up. Don't think for a moment that a wise old buck will tolerate you sending him running too often, but you might get by with one time. On two separate occasions—different years, different areas—I sent big bucks into never-never land after bumping them out of bedding areas early in the pre-rut period. I spotted each of these bucks again within a couple of weeks after they left, however. Of course, I wouldn't want to make a habit of running a trophy buck out of his home range.

One final thought about bucks leaving and returning to the home range: You never know for sure how many mature bucks you spook, and if any of those came back. You can't help leaving human scent behind and making disturbances each time you pass through a hunting area. I truly believe that you must take many more precautionary measures when hunting the pre-rut phase than when hunting the primary or post-rut. During the primary rut, bucks stay on the move, and your main concern then is not spooking the does. During post-rut, the bucks are worn out, which makes them want to stick around in their home ranges unless you really scare them consistently. These bucks, sometimes already in a near nocturnal state of mind, will only get worse if you allow them to detect your presence.

The less nocturnal a buck is, the better the chance you can kill him. I'm sure you already know that. The good news is, during pre-rut a buck often moves during daylight hours, and mature bucks are closer to being diurnal during the primary rut than any other time of year. But the pre-rut only ranks second in the diurnal ratings. Early in the pre-rut period, bucks commonly feed in daylight hours due to the lack of previous hunting pressure and the continuation of summer habits. They need to eat all they can to get ready for the primary rut.

Another good point: During the primary and post-rut periods, you have to be much more selective when choosing ambush locations to remain hidden. It's easy in pre-rut period, when there is plenty of natural camouflage. I also like the ground-hunting opportunities during early autumn, a new and exciting challenge at a time of year when you can use foliage to hide.

I have taken several mature bucks, but I'm most proud of those that I've taken during the pre-rut and post-rut periods. I have discovered the best chances of taking a mature buck in pre-rut occur at two times: One is the first week of the hunting season. The other hot period comes a few weeks later. There is a simple explanation for this. Early in the hunting season, the bucks don't know they are being hunted. Thus, they follow the same habits they did before the hunting began. After the first week of the season, a lapse of opportunity typically occurs. Some hunters take bucks during this dead period of the pre-rut, but the best chance follows two to three weeks after that first week, when the pre-rut frenzy begins. The chapters that follow outline many of the tactics used to take bucks that are still weeks away from kicking the rut into high gear.

Whitetail bucks are creatures of habit in early autumn, often utilizing the same bedding areas, food sources, and trails.

Hunting debuts in most states and provinces as an early archery season in late summer and early fall. This gives bowhunters a good chance to challenge a buck during the pre-rut period. Firearm seasons usually open several weeks later and closer to or during the primary rut, but that doesn't necessarily mean that there are no other windows of opportunity for a gun hunter. Some states and provinces host special hunts with muzzleloader, rifle, or slugster during the heart of the pre-rut season. There are also youth hunts held in early autumn, sometimes before Jack Frost has visited an area. Special hunts with a firearm are common, and although they might be limited to one, two or three days, you can gain an edge if you have an understanding of a buck's habits and the tactics to fool them during the pre-rut period.

I've always been an avid record keeper, tracking the number of deer spotted throughout the season by ambush locations. Surprisingly, on more occasions than not, the records show that I see more deer, including bucks, during the first week of the pre-rut period. I should mention that I'm speaking of averages per efforts hunted. Averages have always been more meaningful than totals.

Personally, I'm glad to be an avid archer just to have the opportunity to hunt hard during pre-rut. True, some bowhunters wait until the cold days of the primary rut to begin hunting. Yet we die-hards love the challenge of hunting the pre-rut while dreaming about the primary rut. Conditions may be less than favorable when hunting early autumn, but if you pattern the animal with a high degree of accuracy, the potential is there to cash in on a bruiser buck. Of course, you must know his whereabouts. ▪

2
Finding the Right Customer

B efore you can begin to think about tactics to fool a mature buck in the pre-rut season, you should know if the right customer exists. Jumping into the pre-rut season with Lady Luck as your guide is seldom productive.

Many hunters talk about shooting only a trophy deer, but waste their time in an area that doesn't have the potential to produce the right customer until the primary rut arrives. Nearly any area is capable of producing a big buck when the breeding begins and I'm sure you know why. However, imagine all your time scouting, selecting and setting up ambush locations, and all the hours you spend hunting that will surely go down the tube if a mature buck isn't, as the old saying goes, ". . . within a mile."

Granted, I believe any time spent in the woods is never wasted. I cherish every moment and opportunity to be out there, even if a big buck isn't within twenty

Hunting for that one mature buck is only possible if you know he's there. If you see him in the pre-rut period before the hunting begins, you have a big buck to pattern.

miles of where I hunt. Nevertheless, if I want to kill one, and I always do, it's in my best interest to know whether he's one mile or twenty miles away.

There are many ways to determine if a big buck exists. I'll cover each aspect and let you decide the best way to find the right customer.

SEEING IS BELIEVING

I'm not going to claim that most folks who shot a big buck knew for sure the deer existed. Nope, most will readily admit that they never saw the deer before. These hunters obviously did things right or they wouldn't have killed the buck. However, it's a known fact that very few hunters identify a certain buck before pursuing it one-on-one.

That doesn't mean that it's not important to see a big buck before the season. On the contrary, if you do see a mature buck, you know he's there and it's up to you to pattern and intercept him.

Seeing a big buck is not necessarily difficult if you hunt an area where they exist. It's really just a matter of having the time to positively make the ID before the hunting begins. There are two ways to accomplish this. One is without ever leaving your vehicle—providing there are access roads in your area and fields that are visible from the roads. If so, set aside several evenings a couple of weeks before the hunting season and plan on covering a few miles.

In late summer, most deer are used to visiting agricultural fields before dusk, since there is no hunting pressure. Even big bucks become habitual, often coming into the same fields near the same locations each evening. Because of warm temperatures, they seldom bed far from the food sources.

Aside from driving roads, you can also park your vehicle and watch a certain field. Many big bucks will enter it and feed only a short time before walking back into cover. If you set up from an advantageous location and watch for an entire evening, you are guaranteed not to miss the action.

If you have fields in the area that are not visible from the road, consider walking into them and setting up. I love these situations, but I can't over emphasize the importance of taking precautionary measures. You will want to set up where you can see a large portion of the field, and particularly the most probable places that deer will come from. However, you must make sure a buck does not detect your presence.

I typically carry in a small stool and set up along the fringes, making certain there is enough foliage around to hide me. I like high points, where my visibility is best, and I always set up where the wind is favorable. Don't take chances if the wind blows your scent into the field and don't set up where deer will come into the field from behind you. You're not out there to be close to a big buck; you only want to confirm that he's around.

Binoculars and spotting scopes are absolutely necessary for identifying the right customer. However, even if you do not see a mature buck before the season debuts, it's not necessarily too late to find one to pattern.

THE PRE-RUT POSITIVE ID

As mentioned in the previous chapter, mature bucks have small home ranges during the pre-rut period. Yet I have spent countless hours before the season in a given area, hoping to see a big buck that I did not see until I started hunting. Hunters often find the right customer only after they spend several hours waiting in ambush. In fact, I often select stand locations that let me continue to watch fields where big bucks might appear.

Naturally, if you see a big buck before the season, you know without a doubt that one is there. But if you don't see a trophy buck in your area, it doesn't mean that one doesn't exist. I can't tell you how many times I went into the pre-rut period discouraged, only to spot a mature buck for the first time a few days after the hunting started.

I mention all this for one reason. I've heard hunters say that if you see a big buck once, you'll never see him again. Wrong! If you see him once, you might not see him again, or you might see him a few times.

What's your chance of seeing a certain buck more than once? The author has found that if you see a buck early in the pre-rut period, chances are good that you could see him again—and again, if you have learned his habits and hunting pressure remains minimal.

Several years ago, while hunting a huge wooded plateau, I saw one buck on four separate occasions. He was easily identifiable by his wide-spread, walnut-colored antlers and short points. I first noticed the buck during the early-archery season and finally shot him during the primary rut, two hundred yards from where I originally picked him out six weeks earlier.

The harder you hunt an area, the less chance you will ever see a mature buck again. I have discovered this major factor more than once. Nevertheless, keep in mind it's always impossible to see the buck on another day, providing someone else doesn't shoot him. That's not out of the question, but during the pre-rut it isn't likely.

SHORT FIREARM SEASONS

Many folks base their chances of killing a big buck on traveling to a certain state or province to hunt. I based most of this book on hunting big bucks that you can pattern in your home range, but there are always those like myself who also enjoy the challenge of patterning and hunting a buck in strange territory. In fact, it's those areas with short gun seasons that often offer the best opportunities, simply because they allow more bucks to grow old.

It's no big secret that fewer bucks are killed in areas where a short firearm season exists. I hunt Illinois each season because the state only has seven days of firearm hunting. There is a three-day season that typi-cally be-gins in primary rut, and a four-day season that follows at the tail-end of the primary rut, or the begin-ning of the post-rut period.

We know that most bucks are killed in the firearm season. In many states, gunners take about eighty percent of the antlered harvest. It's also true that the bulk of the harvest occurs the first few days of the hunting season.

Although lots of factors, such as genetics, nutrition, and buck-to-doe ratio contribute to the number of big bucks in any area, the length of the firearm season and bag limits are a major contributors. In many states and provinces, eighty percent or more of the bucks shot are only one year old.

18

By the way, one-and-one-half-year-old bucks usually make up seventy-five percent or more of the overall antlered harvest in just about every area.

In some states, such as Indiana where I reside, there are sixteen days of a slugster season that usually debuts at about the peak of the rut. Unfortunately, another sixteen days of black-powder hunting follows a short time later. That's thirty-two days of gunning, which drastically reduces the number of bucks that will make it to their second birthday. Other states have similar and even longer firearm seasons, which officials claim are necessary to manage the herd.

Management of a deer herd doesn't always include trophy manage-ment. It's certainly tough on research biologists and other officials making the decisions. They have to manage entire herds, and sometimes it seems that in order to do so, mature bucks can't exist.

That's not to say that hunters always agree with management decisions. It seems that everyone from every state complains about some of them. For instance, I have never agreed with Indiana's summertime problem-deer control permits, or depredating as some call it, which give some landowners and farmers a green light to shoot deer with high-powered rifles, often beginning in late June. The tags they receive (up to ten) are not limited to shooting only antlerless deer, either; I've seen many mature bucks shot before their antlers had fully developed. I'm not sure how many other states have similar summertime depredation programs with high-powered rifles, when only slugsters are allowed in the regular firearm season, but I believe this management practice is in dire need of restructuring.

Some states have done what they can to increase trophy hunting opportunities. Consider that Kentucky went to a one-buck rule a few years ago. Before then, hunters could kill a buck in both the archery and firearm seasons. Now you get one per year. True, there are some dishonest and unethical folks who don't abide by the rule, but it has probably helped Kentucky rank higher in the record books.

No doubt, some states in the Midwest, such as, Illinois, Iowa, Minnesota, and Ohio, put lots of bucks in the record books each year. Every state and province where whitetails roam is capable of producing trophy bucks. You just need to know where to go.

PUBLIC VS. PRIVATE LAND

It's no big secret. Hunters shoot more bucks on private land where little pressure exists than they do on heavily-hunted public land. This doesn't mean you can't kill big bucks on public land. In fact, the pre-rut period is often the best time to shoot a huge buck on public ground. Some bucks always survive the previous hunting season. It might not be many, but it only takes one to make it through a couple of years to offer you potential during the pre-rut.

By the time the primary rut arrives on many public lands, the does and fawns have often been pressured to the point that they have relocated. Thus the bucks have no reason to be there. However, if you are ready to go to work, you can some-times find a mature buck on public land early in the season.

First, consider that not all public grounds are rated equal. Some produce more big bucks than others—particularly those interspersed with numerous tracts of private land. Your chances of success on public land also depend upon how effectively you hunt the area. Tactics differ in pressured areas compared to those where few hunters venture, and the primary difference is that you won't get by with as many mistakes as you might have on private land.

Maps are essential to hunting public lands effectively. One area I used to hunt consistently years ago was always overrun with people, but only in some sections, so I looked for out-of-the-way

Nobody will deny that private land is often better than public land for finding and killing a mature bucks. However, the best chance of doing so on public land occurs early in the pre-rut period, before the hunting pressure intensifies.

places by studying aerial and topographic maps. Actually, what I often discovered was different access routes. Maps allowed me to get into and out of an area with fewer disturbances than I would have otherwise, and they helped me to select ambush sites close to and sometimes bordering private properties, where the least hunting pressure occurred. This is a crucial strategy for hunting public land.

As mentioned in this book's introduction, these tactics are based on hunting "smart" deer...deer that have sharp survival instincts. They learn fast, and they know when they are being hunted. To a smart deer, it really doesn't matter if it's public or private land. He only wants to be where he feels the safest.

With this said, I would still recommend you hunt private land if possible, but be aware, not all private land is created equal either. The public area I mentioned earlier was really a getaway for me from some heavily-hunted private land that offered little or no trophy hunting potential for the same reason some public land doesn't. Too many people going in and out.

But let's don't kid ourselves. We all know that quality private land offers great opportunities for taking big bucks; the biggest problem is gaining access to quality private land. Every year it seems landowners are more reluctant to grant permission. It's also true that each day, more and more large tracts of land are broken into smaller parcels. Still, if you work hard enough, it could pay off.

Always know the area before asking a landowner for permission to hunt. The better you have learned boundaries and landmarks before asking, the better your chance of getting in. Plat maps are helpful, since they show both boundaries and owners' names. (You should always know the name of the person you talk to.) You can usually purchase a plat map at a nearby title office.

I have spent countless hours studying maps and making inquiries just to learn all I can about property I want to hunt. I've also found that your chances of getting permission fluctuate from area to area. In some places it seems almost everyone will let you hunt. In other places, nobody will let you hunt no matter how well prepared you are.

No doubt, you usually have a better chance of finding the right buck on private land. That's the bottom line. It's not necessarily the best news for deer hunters, but it remains a fact.

Leasing land is another option and certainly worth considering if you want to pursue big bucks. I'm not really for or against. In some ways I hate to see hunters leasing land because it takes opportunities away from all others. Nonetheless, who can blame someone for doing it? If it's a big buck that you want, buying or leasing land can help you get the job done.

Several years ago, I said that money could put you onto the biggest bucks. That is still true today. There are guides and outfitters, and there are landowners who will gladly trade you antlered bucks for green bucks. I'm not talking about fenced hunts, a form of hunting I'm absolutely opposed to. I'm speaking of quality areas, sometimes managed for producing mature bucks, that only large funds will get you into. However, even these areas seldom offer guarantees. Some sell too many hunts, and the pressure produces fewer big bucks by moving them out or into nocturnal hiding. The good news, though, is that the pre-rut period is sometimes the best time to hunt on pressured private land. Like pressured public land, you get the jump on others by trying to pattern a big buck before the breeding begins.

GENETICS AND NUTRITION

I'm not so sure anyone knows which is more important for growing big bucks—genetics or nutrition. Researchers have argued about it for years, and some assert it's 50-50. One qualified researcher said genetics mean almost nothing if the bucks don't have nutrition.

Personally, I like having both. I'm fortunate to do most of my hunting in agricultural areas where nutritional foods are common. I'm fortunate, too, to hunt where any buck has the potential to grow big antlers because it's in the bloodline.

You can't do anything about genetics. The right genes are either there, or not. If you have the land, though, you can do something about nutrition with food plots. The right food not only increases antler size—there are several good books out there about using nutrition to produce big antlers—but also provides increased hunting opportunities.

Soil varies from one area to another, which is exactly why some areas grow better antlers. I've seen bottomlands that are crawling with huge-racked bucks, even though they are hunted extensively.

A few hours drive from my home is Muscatatuck National Wildlife Refuge, a region that contains a diversity of rich bottomlands, including croplands, woods and marshes. Whopper bucks have been coming out of this area since it was first hunted in the 1980s. Granted, there are not as many big bucks as there used to be because officials control the area's deer herd each year with random-draw hunts. However, surviving bucks still grow huge antlers because of the soil itself.

Soils with minerals and high pH levels are strong contributors to growing big bucks. That's precisely why so many bucks in the record books come from the Midwest. You can't do much about woodlands, but if you own land or manage it, you can improve soil fertility, adding fertilizers and lime to increase pH levels of agricultural fields. Make no mistake, though, you can't beat areas that already have the soil it takes for growing big bucks.

Some areas have never produced a lot of big bucks and they never will. There are plenty of reasons, ranging from too many does and bucks harvested, to poor genetics and/or food. As mentioned previously, though, there's always that one big buck out there, if you can just find him.

TRACKS AND CLUES

Unfortunately, you can never determine (with certainty) that a trophy buck left the sign you found. Consider tracks. I have studied tracks for a number of years and, except for size, I have never found a positive way of telling a buck from a doe track. Moreover, even though some tracks are large and *probably* made by a buck, you can't say for sure that the track was made by a buck with big antlers.

A couple of years ago, my wife Vikki, shot a seven-point buck. He was a beautiful deer and a fine trophy for any bowhunter. The early-season deer field-dressed at 170 pounds and had huge feet that left huge tracks, but his antlers were nothing exceptional.

Only in snow have I been able to tell the difference between a buck track and a doe track. Bucks usually leave drag marks about one to one-and-one-half feet long in shallow snow, while does do not, seeming to walk a little daintier than bucks. However, in deeper snow, usually four inches or more, all deer leave drag marks.

This rub was probably made from a buck whose image was captured on a motion-activated camera that was set up not far from this location. *Photo by Fiduccia Enterprises.*

Rubs do provide some indication of antler size, which I'll discuss in a later chapter. Of course, right after bucks lose their velvet they usually rub only small saplings. This all changes without warning as the pre-rut season progresses, however.

One final word about finding the right customer: Remember that the antlers of bucks in velvet often look bigger than they will after the velvet is gone. That's not to say that you would have problems identifying a big buck before he sheds velvet, but sometimes small and typical eight-point frames can fool you. If you want to hunt big bucks, it's important that you know one when you see one. ■

3
Sizing Them Up

K nowing a trophy buck when you see one is not always difficult. That is, assuming you can examine the antlers in a taxidermy studio. On the hoof, however, you must be close to the buck and have him plainly visible for a given period. Now let's get back to reality. In most situations, you have only seconds to field judge a buck's antlers. Moreover, he's usually in brush or hardwoods.

Consider a buck I shot at one year before writing this chapter. After retrieving my spent arrow, I climbed back in the stand and thought about what had happened thirty minutes earlier. The buck had slowly approached me but, with each step he took, I remained unsure about his credentials. I was hunting southern Illinois, and with the peak rut still several days away, I had hoped to cash in on a buck that would have a Boone and Crockett score of 140 inches or more. Shooting the eight-pointer was questionable. My rushed shot and indecisiveness probably contributed to my

Many times, you get only seconds to size up a buck's antlers. Instead of focusing on the entire rack, concentrate on a portion of the antlers that is most visible. *Photo by Vikki L. Trout.*

miss, and I sat wondering just what the buck would have really scored. He was close to what I hoped for, but there had been some doubt.

Then there are bucks that don't create doubts. Such was the case during the firearm season just two weeks later, when I saw a buck and knew I wanted him. He scored right at 140 inches.

Despite the odds against you, it is possible to judge antlers quickly with some degree of accuracy. To do so, you only need to concentrate on the factors that contribute greatly to the overall score of the buck . . . and always reconsider your first spur-of-the-moment judgment when trying to size him up.

AVOID FATAL ERRORS

Shooting the wrong buck is one way to make certain you won't get a crack at the right buck. However, first let me point out that a trophy buck is, as they say, "in the eyes of the beholder."

The overall score and number of points may or may not have anything to do with what you hope to shoot. For this reason, each individual should set his limitations before the hunting begins. It's true that we put a lot of emphasis on trophy hunting today, but it's also true that there are more deer, and more opportunities than there have ever been to take a trophy. The key is to shoot a buck that will make you happy, and not to wait on one that will impress others.

There are times when you can be easily fooled, and believe me I have been there and done that. The worst thing you can do is shoot a buck that you don't want. However, filling a tag, regardless of what the antlers score, should always be a proud moment.

Many hunters do not want to shoot a buck that does not qualify for the Pope and Young and Boone and Crockett Club, or another organization with minimum entry levels. Most who pursue big bucks do focus on the mini-mum score. To accurately estimate the minimum score of bucks on the hoof, you should first spend time at a taxidermy studio.

I look at it this way: Allow your first impression to guide you. If you have a positive first impression, you will know it's the buck you want. If your first impression leaves doubts, it is probably not the buck you hoped for. More than likely you will know it when the right buck comes along, and you can avoid making a fatal error.

TALL AND NARROW VS. SHORT AND WIDE

For just a moment, forget about the number of points and antler mass, both of which contribute greatly to the overall score. You can get a good idea if a buck is record-book potential with only a quick glance of the antlers. If the deer is coming towards you or walking away, you can determine if the buck has a tall and narrow rack, or short and wide antlers.

Deer with tall, narrow antlers almost always score higher than those with a large inside spread and short points. Consider that a significant inside spread looks impressive, but it does little for the overall score. Naturally, a buck with a spread of eighteen inches is only three inches better than one with a spread of fifteen inches. On the other hand, nearly every point adds to the score when a buck carries tall antlers.

My best whitetail grossed about 158 inches. His inside spread was only fifteen and one-half inches, but several of his tines were better than ten inches. I've taken bucks with considerably more width, but none has scored as much. With this in mind, most of us would hope to encounter a buck with tall antlers and considerable width. Unfortunately, such a phenomenon seldom occurs.

JUDGING SPREAD

When some hunters discuss bucks they see, they often make comments such as, "He was only about fifteen inches wide." I don't mind telling you, I've seen lots of super bucks with antlers only fifteen to sixteen inches wide, including one on my wall that taped out a little under 160 gross inches.

I've already mentioned the insignificance of antler spread, but who can deny that wide antlers look impressive on the wall? This is precisely why some hunters consider width before shooting a buck.

Surprisingly, you can estimate the spread of the antlers easily. It's done by comparing them to the ears. When a deer's ears are not laid back and are upright

If a buck's antlers are as wide as his ears, he will have an inside spread of about fifteen inches. The antlers of this buck stick out several inches past the ears. He will probably have a wide spread of twenty to twenty-two inches.

and outwards, they are about fifteen inches from tip-to-tip. Thus, if the tips of the antlers are equal to the tips of the ears, you can safely assume the buck has an inside spread of about fifteen inches.

If the antlers are wider than the ears, consider how much further they extend. A buck that has one and one-half inches of antler past each ear would have a spread of about eighteen inches. Bucks that have a spread of twenty inches or more are rare and much more difficult to estimate, but if time allows and the deer faces into you or walks away, you can estimate the spread with a high degree of accuracy.

TOTAL POINTS

The number of points contributes greatly to the score. It's difficult for an eight-pointer to surpass the Pope and Young minimum score of 125, much less the minimum Boone & Crockett score of 170. Moreover, when discussing a big buck, a ten-pointer sounds better than an eight-pointer. Al-though most trophy hunters would not pass up an eight-point buck with large headgear to wait on something with more points, there is satisfaction in knowing that a buck carries at least eight points.

To judge the total number of points, you need only to have a side view of one antler and focus on the number of points coming off the main beam. For instance, if you see two points coming off the main beam, the buck is probably an eight-pointer. You are seeing the G-2 and G-3 points. You can assume the buck will have a brow tine on each side. The brow tine, G-2, G-3, and end of the main beam total

The total number of points can be estimated by the number of points you see pointing up. An eight-pointer will typically have two points up.

four points. If the buck carries an even rack, he is an eight-pointer. If you see three points up, the buck is probably a ten-pointer. Sticker points and other short points are not usually seen, but that's good news when you shoot a buck. There are times when a buck will have a broken or missing brow tine, but just as often there is an additional point you didn't count on.

Previously I mentioned the 140-inch buck I shot during the firearm season last year. When I saw the buck, he was walking broadside. I could easily see a G-2 and G-3, and there was little doubt the buck was an eight-pointer. When I walked up to the downed deer, though, I found he was an eight-pointer with a broken brow tine. That reduced the buck's overall score by four inches.

THE BROW TINE CONTRIBUTION

Few hunters realize the importance of brow tines when estimating the overall score of the antlers. Although some bucks have more than two brow tines, most do not, and short brow tines can reduce the score considerably. I've seen several whopper bucks that had long points, but short brow tines.

Although it's difficult to determine beam length, total points and mass when you see a buck coming toward you, you will often see brow tines. Many hunters seldom think about them, but brow tines are often the real sleepers when you want to identify a mature or trophy buck.

Trophy bucks need long brow tines to score high. Mature bucks often grow long brow tines, even when the other points and main beams are short. As for overall score, consider this: A buck with short brow tines of two inches each, adds four inches to his total score. One with six-inch brow tines adds twelve points to the score. The eight-inch difference is major when it comes to clicking the total score button. It's much more difficult to see brow tines than points if a buck isn't close, but traditionally those with mass have longer brow tines.

MAIN BEAMS AND MASS

Judging the mass of an antler is probably more difficult than deter-mining the length of brow tines. However, make no mistake that mass plays an important role in the buck's overall score, simply because the circumference of an antler is measured in four locations. A buck that has considerable mass could add one inch or more at each location where a measurement is taken.

Typically, most hunters (myself included) cannot estimate mass in inches with a high degree of accuracy. However, spindly racks do look considerably different than massive antlers. The whiter the antlers, the easier it is to determine, but sometimes white antlers will fool you just because they show up better. If time allows, look at the base of the antler near the brow tine, the best location for identifying a massive antler.

The length of the main beams is also important, and one antler can be estimated if you have a broadside view of the buck. There is usually very little difference in the length of both antlers. If one is twenty-two inches, more than likely the other will be between twenty-one to twenty-three inches.

If you notice a main beam that extends to almost the end of the deer's nose, it is a long beam, probably twenty-four inches or more. Nevertheless, that's not to say you should wait on a buck with an antler that extends to the tip of the buck's nose. If you do, you're in for a long wait. Many record-book whitetails have only eighteen and nineteen-inch main beams. Normally, if I see a main beam that extends two-thirds of the way to the buck's nose, I can be certain it has long main beams. However, some trophy bucks have main beams twenty-two inches and

Although judging the score of a buck's antlers is a guessing game, many individuals can do so within a couple of inches. The bigger the buck's rack, though, the more difficult the guessing becomes.

longer, yet they extend only halfway to the deer's nose. Those with wide inside spreads simply grow more outward than forward.

BODY CLUES

Surprisingly, it is possible for a young buck to carry big antlers. That won't matter to some hunters who are happy with large headgear. However, those who want to shoot only a mature buck won't be happy with pulling the trigger on a young buck with respectable antlers. Thus, you should consider body clues that might separate the old timers from the young bucks.

As mentioned previously, the better the antlers show up, the smaller the body looks. It's similar to how I've judged the head size of black bears. With bears, the bigger the body, the smaller the head appears. However, that doesn't necessarily mean the skull will not score high. It only means that the large body dwarfs the head.

Similarly, the antlers of a large-bodied buck might appear smaller at first glance. The question is, does body size have anything to do with the age of a buck?

The answer is both yes and no. Yes, a mature buck could very well be the biggest-bodied buck in your area. For this reason, if you are a good judge when it comes to estimating weight, it might be safe to believe that a buck with a huge body is a mature one. Note that I said "might."

Consider that, as the rut progresses, bucks lose a considerable amount of body weight. Terrain, as well as the time of year you see him, will dictate how much weight a buck loses when he covers ground in

Being indecisive when a buck approaches can be costly. If you have no doubt that the buck you see is the one you have waited for, he probably is.

search of does. You can assume that any buck sighted during the rut, or post rut, was several pounds heavier at one time.

Overall length is another matter. Long-bodied bucks are usually mature bucks. Determining that a buck has a long body is not necessarily easy, but one thing is for sure: Bucks don't get shorter as they get older.

A few years ago during the late archery season, I spotted four bucks together. Seeing several at once wasn't unusual, considering the rut had ended six weeks earlier. All four passed by me fifty yards away and I could see that one had a huge eight-point rack while another had a little bigger ten-point set of headgear. The eight-pointer though, was much longer than the ten-point, and I suspected he was the older of the two.

Most mature bucks are grayer and darker in the face than young bucks. The white patch on the throat varies in contrast from buck to buck, but I've never noticed it had anything to do with the age of a buck, and white circles around the eyes should not be confused with gray. It's the gray hair (in some cases almost black) on the sides of the face that provide some indication you are seeing a mature buck.

It's a close call when it comes to judging a buck's age by his body, although it's true that the buck with the biggest body is probably the most mature. If this isn't possible to compare one buck to another, and it usually isn't, you must try to determine the deer's length and height.

A Helping Hand?

There is no doubt that the right binocular will provide a helping hand when estimating the size of antlers. However, in the wrong area, a binocular might cost you a shooting opportunity. For instance, when I hunt dense areas, even a quality optic device is a handicap. It takes time to find the deer and time is costly when minimum visibility exists.

In dense thickets and hardwoods, I seldom pack a binocular along, preferring to rely on my eyes to make a timely decision. On the other hand, when hunting near a food plot where visibility is not a factor, I never regret being equipped with a binocular.

Hunter Cody Fiduccia and his guide Alex glass an animal carefully to decide if it has the type of antlers they are looking for. Both binoculars offer good light gathering qualities—which is a crucial element to see game animals during low light conditions like dawn and dusk. *Photo by Fiduccia Enterprises.*

Compact binoculars are popular with whitetail hunters because they are less cumbersome and easier to steady, but there is more to the story. With a compact binocular, you will have to sacrifice objective diameter. The larger the diameter of lens, the easier you can find your target, which is why my preference for whitetails is an 8 X binocular with an objective diameter of 32mm. Although they are not compact, they are lightweight, easy to handle, and have a rubberized finish to prevent slipping. Finally, you will want a binocular that does well in low light, reduces glare and, if affordable, is also waterproof and fogproof.

Although some individuals can estimate the size of antlers better than others, everyone can be fooled on the right day. It's like putting together a big puzzle. I find it challenging, even in the taxidermy studio, and I'm often way off, even when

I have all the time necessary to study the rack. Generally, the bigger the antlers, the more difficult it is to estimate the score of the buck.

As for the eight-point buck mentioned at the beginning of this story, I do have a good idea what he scored. My wife, Vikki, found one of his sheds the next spring, easily recognizable by the long and perfectly straight G-2 point of his left antler (I had studied the left antler as the buck approached). The left antler measured fifty-four inches. If the right antler measured equally with the left (it was never located although we thoroughly searched the area) and the buck had an inside spread of sixteen inches, I can estimate his overall score was 124 inches.

In ending this chapter, let me say that each individual should shoot the buck that makes them the happiest. You should not base your decision on that of another hunter.

Perhaps there is too much emphasis put on shooting mature and trophy bucks today. It's also true that I have just contributed to this theory by discussing the methods herein for recognizing the right buck when you see him. However, I can't deny that the challenge of deer hunting has led many of us to shooting that one certain buck. The factors mentioned are techniques to consider when reading the tactics that follow. ▪

4

Autumn Hotspots

ecause bucks cover so much ground during the primary rut in search of does, patterning them is practically impossible. During any portion of the pre-rut period, however, bucks visit certain food sources consistently. If hunters are aware of those foods that will attract deer, they have the opportunity to pattern and kill the bucks they want. But beware—food sources can change as quickly as the temperature can drop.

We often fail to recognize the buck's need to feed regularly during the pre-rut period, especially during those four to five weeks before the peak of the rut. This is the common scenario since a buck knows he will soon be busy doing everything but eating.

Every geographical area supports different whitetail foods that become available during the early archery season.

During the pre-rut period, bucks feed heavily to strengthen themselves for the primary rut.

Whether you hunt in farmlands or big timber, the more you are aware of and the better you know the various types of trees, foliage, and crops in your area, the easier it is for you to locate those food sources that attract the bucks.

AGRICULTURAL FOODS

A few years ago, I moved a stand deeper into a funnel connected to a crop field, hoping a buck would pass by as it traveled to a bedding area. The first time I hunted the area, I spotted a young buck. A short time later, a respectable ten-pointer, which I had spotted weeks earlier in a lush soybean field, followed the young buck's

The author took this ten-pointer during the pre-rut period as it traveled a corridor away from a harvested cornfield. He had seen the buck on one previous occasion. *Photo by Vikki L. Trout.*

trail. My Muzzy broadhead zipped cleanly through the deer's vitals and he traveled less than one hundred yards before piling up.

The most interesting thing about that encounter, which occurred only about one week before the primary rut got underway, was how and why the buck ended up in front of my stand. Like many bucks visiting agricultural food sources, he had been feeding in the fields frequently during late summer before dusk, only to vanish into the countryside in the following weeks.

An agricultural field is often the limelight of the early season for many pre-rut season hunters. Alfalfa and clover along with soybeans and corn are usually favorites. However, much of your success near these fields depends upon the time harvesting occurs and whether or not bucks will reach the fields in daylight hours. The ten-point buck mentioned previously was no longer coming to the agricultural fields during daylight hours. I had to utilize a trail to intercept him.

When I hunted in the Bow Zone of Alberta several years ago, bucks commonly visited agricultural fields in daylight. There was little or no hunting pressure, which made it possible to set up along the fields or even in draws in the middle of them if necessary. In many areas though, seasoned bucks won't enter open fields until darkness prevails.

Most green fields are attractive to whitetails in autumn, including succulent alfalfa, clover, and some manufactured food plots. Winter wheat and a few other types of green foliage are better wintertime foods. (I discuss them in more detail in the post-rut section of this book.) Soybeans, if still green, are often the whitetail's favorite during early autumn because they offer a high dosage of protein.

Some agricultural fields are like magnets to all deer in autumn. However, the best possibility of intercepting a mature buck often occurs early in the pre-rut period, before he is aware of hunting pressure.

Unfortunately, in some areas, many soybean fields are no longer green when the early season hunting begins. But even a recently harvested soybean field will attract bucks if other foods are not available.

While looking for hot agricultural food sources, be open-minded. For example, cornfields often appeal to hunters only after harvesting, although harvested cornfields usually only attract deer for a short time. However, standing cornfields can be long-term buck magnets, depending upon the amount of waste corn. Bucks will commonly switch to another field two to three weeks after the harvest, yet feed and hide out in cornfields for as long as the corn remains standing.

It doesn't take long for the bucks to find a harvested cornfield. Typically, they will be there within twenty-four hours. In fact, the best hunting often occurs the first few days following the harvest.

Although clover and alfalfa don't attract many deer after hard freezes, I love hunting these fields in early autumn, when they offer an opportunity to ambush a buck.

Always use logic when setting up a stand near an agricultural food source. In other words, don't place a

Soybeans are high in protein and although green soybeans are rare in early autumn, if you find them you can probably count on the spot to attract several deer, and possibly a mature buck. *Photo by Vikki L. Trout.*

37

stand along the fringe where you are totally exposed when leaving the area, and always plan your ambush in a location that lets you come and go with the least chance of deer detecting your presence. Hunting an agricultural field will be productive only if you can keep a mature buck from knowing you are there. That's easier said than done, but absolutely necessary for pre-rut success.

The final consideration with any agricultural field is mast and hunting pressure. If a buck knows you are there, you can forget about killing him close to the field. Even if he doesn't know you are there, he will probably prefer to feed in seclusion if mast is available.

HOT OAKS

Acorns have always been a food source for a number of wildlife species. The whitetail is no exception, and this autumn delight could also be your ticket to a trophy buck. Remember, too, that acorns are extremely high in protein and preferred by mature bucks looking toward the anxiety of breeding.

Hunting near the oaks has now become a tradition for me. Several other deer hunters also rely on this tactic to outsmart a buck in the pre-rut period. Unfortunately, though, there is more to succeeding than just setting up a stand in an area of hardwoods where the acorns are falling. The number of available acorns, the types of oaks producing them, and the location of the trees all play a key role in your chances of success.

Oaks are abundant throughout North America, with more than fifty species in the white and red oak families. Although many of them produce acorns, deer often prefer the acorns of the white oak family which, according to many whitetail experts, is because white oak acorns are sweeter than red oak. The more bitter red oak acorns do not usually become a food source for the deer until late in the pre-rut season, or in the winter and post-rut period. However, exceptions do occur when the white oak mast fails.

A few years ago, I found no white oak acorns in an area I frequently hunt, a stand of hardwoods that usually produces each year. This year's production had been affected by a late frost in April. A few red oaks did produce, though, and became a magnet to deer passing through. So although you can safely assume that white oaks will draw the deer first if the choice is offered, you can also bet that any acorn-producing oak, regardless of its species, will attract deer if they are the only acorns around.

You can determine which type of oak you are looking at by examining the leaves. Those in the white oak family have leaves with rounded lobes, whereas red oak leaves have bristled, pointed lobes. There is also a distinct difference in the bark of the two groups, and with experience, you will probably be able to identify the type of oak you are approaching without needing to examine the leaves.

Acorns, particularly the sweeter nuts of white oaks, commonly attract mature bucks during the pre-rut period. Those in secluded areas offer the best opportunity for a big buck to be there in daylight hours.

Proper identification of the oaks may be necessary if you hope to am-bush a buck that is feeding on acorns, and a good field book on the subject can provide excellent illustrations of both the white and red oak families. There's much more to it than just finding acorns on the ground.

Since the acorn crop can change from one mile to another, droppings provide the best indication of which oaks the deer prefer. The nut mast is usually affected by spring and summer weather and can vary in only a short distance. A late frost, for example, may affect the number of acorns in any given area. In addition, a drought will also be significant.

You may also gain knowledge of the acorn mast by watching fields that whitetails commonly visit. If these fields are deserted, even when little or no hunting pressure exists, you can probably assume that the nut mast has intercepted the deer. I've often hunted an agricultural field only to see deer stop coming to it without warning—a good indication that the acorns have started hitting the ground.

Sometimes, though, the fewer acorns available, the better. Nothing makes the hunting tougher than too many acorns. When and if almost every oak celebrates a banner year, the deer can feed along many of the trails and do not need to congregate in any given area. That makes hunting mature bucks more difficult.

You already know that deer are browsers—not grazers. Even if very few oaks shed acorns, the deer may feed for only a short period before moving on. However, they return more frequently when they have fewer acorns to choose from.

When looking for hot oaks, I concentrate on finding the food source and don't look for hot trails. Looking for a trail riddled with tracks is one of the biggest mistakes a hunter can make in the pre-rut period. It's much better to stick with the food source where the buck will end up. Later, I'll discuss other key factors for locating pre-rut season buck trails and rubs, but these areas do not compare to finding that one certain oak that has produced a heavy nut mast when other oaks fail.

The fewer the acorns, the better it is to pattern a buck and know where he will be. If several oaks produce, a buck could be anywhere.

When deer visit an oak regularly, they will leave sign similar to turkey scratchings. However, a major difference is plainly visible. Turkeys scratch large areas, often clearing up to one foot or more of debris from the woods' floor. The whitetail moves only a small portion of leaves to find an acorn.

Some hunters believe that deer paw the ground to get to acorns, but they actually use their nose to locate the acorn and then scoot the leaves away to grab it, leaving depressions in the leaves that are only a few inches around. Deer do paw the ground to get to food under shallow snow, and to move snow away to bed down.

Those oaks in the thickest cover usually provide the best opportunities. This is true with all secluded food sources, and is more advantageous to you. Acorns in dense areas mean the buck is more likely to be there in daylight hours. The last five minutes of daylight in the evening or the first minutes of pink morning light may be when he arrives at the oaks growing amidst thick cover.

Keep in mind, no oak will continue shedding acorns for a long period during the pre-rut season. Some begin shedding their acorns long before the first frost while others will not drop until freezing temperatures or a strong wind occurs. The time that acorns are dropping depends on the number of acorns and how quickly they fall. Eventually, the supply is exhausted.

I have found some oaks will provide hunting opportunities for two or three weeks. Others may be hot for only a matter of days. For this reason, you must stay on top of things consistently, checking for fresh sign and the number of acorns you see on the ground. Once the nuts stop falling, it is time to move on. Another food source might be attracting the deer.

OTHER FOODS

Don't think for a moment that only acorns will attract a mature buck. It could be that a certain oak in the area is the hottest item on the list, but there are usually other options for a buck to consider.

Two favorites are persimmons and crab apples. Both fruits are timed perfectly for the introduction of the pre-rut period and both have the capability of attracting a trophy buck.

A major factor, though, could be the location of the food source. Those in secluded areas do the best, for all the same reasons as do the hidden oaks. However, like the oaks, the mast of persimmons and crab apples is dependent upon weather.

Many years ago, I took a super eight-pointer near a crab apple tree during the first week of the archery season. The tree was located in an area of numerous dogwoods and close to several small hills laced in thick Virginia pines and dense honeysuckle. The pine and honeysuckle provided bedding, and the crab apples had probably become the buck's first stopping point when he left his bedding area.

I had never seen the buck previously and had pinned my hopes of seeing a mature buck come to the crab apples totally upon several gouged trees and big tracks. The second time I hunted the area he showed up, about thirty minutes before dusk. Today, he hangs on my living-room wall.

Understand that crab apples don't last long. They fall to the ground quickly and lots of other animals are attracted to them. So they might provide action of one week or less.

Domestic apple trees are occasionally more dependable than crab apples for attracting a mature buck in autumn, providing they are in the right location. The same goes for wild and domestic pears. The drawback is whether you can hunt these foods even if they are available in your hunting areas. Many are located in open areas and won't tempt a mature buck until after dark.

Persimmons are quite common throughout much of North America, typically ripening during the pre-rut period. Once they ripen and start falling to the ground (usually after the first frost), deer begin visiting them. They also are reliable during the pre-rut for an extended period because they don't all fall to the ground in a matter of days, as do some other fruit and nut trees. Nevertheless, like the oaks, the fewer persimmon trees that produce, the easier it becomes to pattern a mature buck.

I hunt one forty-acre tract in Illinois that is laced with persimmon trees, and different ones produce fruit each year, making it difficult to pattern a big buck. Yet in one area of Indiana where I also hunt, there are only a couple of persimmon trees. They don't always produce fruit, but when they do, I know the food source that is most likely to attract a dominant buck.

Crab apples and persimmons are among the other autumn foods that might allow you to pattern a buck during the pre-rut period

Dogwood berries are another food source to consider during autumn. Dogwoods are usually found throughout a given area, but it is a dogwood thicket that offers the most potential for ambushing a mature buck if there are enough of the small, nutritious berries available. Usually though, I prefer to hunt near dogwoods only when the oaks, persimmons, and other common fruit trees fail.

Each hunter should become familiar with the area he hunts to see what attracts the deer, since several foods can increase your chance of intercepting a mature buck in the pre-rut period. If a particular food attracts does and fawns, it might also attract a mature buck. However, before the primary rut, the older bucks love visiting an out-of-the-way food source where few other deer will venture.

SECLUDED AMBUSH LOCATIONS

I have often compared hunting near secluded foods to hunting black bear over baits. Granted, there are major differences, but one factor is very important. The closer you set up to the food source, the better the chance of getting a shooting opportunity. Of course, when setting a bait for bear, I can choose a perfect ambush location. When hunting the secluded foods for that certain trophy whitetail, I must accept the buck's terrain that is available. Normally, though, I will place my stand in a tree close to the food source and avoid the trails leading to and from. After all, this is where the buck will soon be. He may come from any given direction when approaching, but he is much more likely to offer a shooting opportunity and be spotted in daylight hours if you hunt close to the food source.

Portable stands are beneficial simply because you can leave them set up at the secluded food source. I can place my stand and sneak in and out with only the sound of my approach and departure through the leaves. How-ever, you must check wind direction from your stand and hunt only when it is favorable. Like I've said before, it takes only one goof to change a buck's habits.

Hunting by a food source is no different from hunting along trails. You simply must be there often and give your tactics a chance to work. Deciding which time of day is best—morning or evening—will depend on the location of the bedding area as well as other available foods. I've always believed that the closer the food source is to the bedding area, the more likely it is that the buck will show up when the sun shines. However, one thing is certain: You should hunt both periods of the day if you hope to cash in on a trophy buck. The more you are there, the more likely you are to see the buck that has visited the food source.

Although I often spot does and fawns coming to secluded foods late in the mornings and early in the afternoons, this is seldom true of bucks. The bucks are prone to show up in the early part of the morning and/or during the low light of the evening. Often, your best chance of intercepting a mature buck will occur just before you leave in the evenings.

The hunter can choose from an array of hunting tactics during the pre-rut period. Just ask my good friend, Dean Stallion who, in 1999, took a super buck early in the pre-rut period just before dusk. Stallion was set up near a probable bedding area and a waterhole (a drought was in progress) when the 189-inch buck appeared.

Hunting by a food source is only one pre-rut tactic, but often the best way to pattern a mature buck. But bear in mind, this tactic often dies quickly because the food source always expires, and before it does, you can bet that your presence will eventually arouse suspicion and change a buck's habits. Fortunately, there are other pre-rut hunting options to consider when the food sources fail. ▩

.

5
Pay-Off Rubs

Many hunters say that rubs only tell you where a buck has been, and provide no indication as to where he may be or and will soon be. These same hunters claim that scrapes are much more reliable for ambushing a buck. Wrong! As I'll discuss in a later chapter, some scrapes are productive. However, I have never found the hottest scrapes to offer more potential for killing a mature buck than certain rubs. On the contrary, I've taken far more bucks along rub lines than near the best scrapes.

It's true that, like all buck sign you discover, rubs are after-the-fact evidence. They tell you where a buck once stood and what he had on his mind. But there's a whole lot more to the story. Many pre-rut rubs are sign-posts that a buck will visit repeatedly. That's not to say he makes it a point to return to a certain rub, but many a hunter has ambushed a buck by knowing which rubs he would pass by repeatedly.

Make no mistake: Bucks make rubs throughout the entire period that they carry hardened antlers. But those rubs that offer the best hunting opportunities are made during the pre-rut and post-rut periods, and the former period is the most reliable.

Nevertheless, like all rut-hunting tactics that I'm aware

Bucks become violent as the pre-rut period gets closer to the primary rut. These isolated rubs are often only sporadic rubs and do not mean a buck will return.

45

of, there's a catch. Setting up an ambush post near the first buck rubs you come across during the pre-rut period could result in many mornings and afternoons of boredom. The fact, is some rubs got it, and some don't.

First and foremost, you should understand that two types of rubs exist. 1) Sporadic rubs. 2) Rub lines. You will find more No. 1 rubs than No. 2 rubs, but they are less likely to produce action.

Sporadic rubs, found here and there, never connect to one another and occur for various reasons. For instance, bucks randomly rub trees upon removing their velvet and just after, which often leads to several rubs in a circle of thirty-yards, or larger. While photographing whitetails and spending countless hours watching them, I've seen bucks rub trees just because they suddenly turned vicious, usually the result of another buck nearby, or perhaps a doe that wasn't quite ready. Sometimes a buck rubs a tree simply because he feels like doing it at a given moment. Either way, this sort of action causes sporadic rubbing.

The question of just why deer rub trees is still argued amongst hunters and researchers. However, I believe there are several reasons for the behavior. Rubbing removes dead skin. It builds neck muscles. It provides a signpost of scent from the forehead gland as the buck tries toward off rivals or even attract does. It also provides a method for releasing anger and aggression. Undoubtedly, rubs serve other purposes that we are unaware of, too.

We know that bucks like to rub aromatic trees and those that hold scent, but not always. Yet which trees they choose to rub often depends upon what is available. In the wild, I seldom see a dogwood tree rubbed, although they are plentiful in almost every area I hunt. Captive deer will almost always rub dogwood trees if they are available. It's also true that bucks don't usually rub trees with lots of low limbs, preferring those with straight trunks at least three feet up from the ground. Some of their favorites are pines, cedars, and maples.

Although many bucks may rub the same tree, don't think for a moment that a buck returns to a certain tree just so he can rub. Nope, rubs are not like scrapes. In other words, a buck could care less about returning to a particular tree just to tear it up or leave his scent.

Personally, I really don't care that much about why a buck rubs a tree, nor do I care much about which trees he is likely to rub. From a hunting standpoint, I'm more concerned about those that were rubbed by a mature buck, and which ones he will likely come back to on another day.

Research indicates that mature bucks do most of the rubbing during the pre-rut period. However, don't take those findings too seriously. Little bucks don't mind knocking the daylights out of a tree several weeks before the primary rut. I've witnessed this many times while photographing whitetails and while hunting. I might add, some of these trees rubbed by little bucks had not been hit previously but after viewing them you would swear that a monster buck got hold of the tree.

Research also indicates a correlation between a buck's age and the size of the tree he rubs. Mature bucks love to rub big trees. That's a fact. However, don't take this statement too seriously either, since research deals with the majority, not the exception to the rules. In reality, little bucks occasionally rub big trees and big bucks sometimes rub little trees (if you define a big tree as one with a diameter of three inches or more). For the records, you should never look at research as a golden rule. We're still in the early stages of the science and nature of whitetails, and we can often learn more from personal experiences—than research.

Several weeks before the primary rut, you won't find many large trees rubbed. As the pre-rut period draws closer to the primary rut, bigger rubbed trees become more noticeable. Nevertheless, this only means that some small rubbed trees could be the work of a mature buck as well as a young buck.

Probably the most important clue about whether a rub is the work of a mature buck or a youngster is the damage to the tree. Several bucks could rub the same tree. In fact, because scent remains on some trees for several days, or even weeks, a buck may be compelled to rub them mainly because another did. That's providing he passes the rub and scents it. As I said previously, bucks don't make a habit of

Mature bucks rub both small and large trees. However, trees with deep gouges on any size trees indicate the works of a buck with large headgear.

47

A rub line might be followed from one hundred yards to one-fourth mile or further. The distance between rubs varies. One rub might be visible from another, or might not.

visiting a certain rub for the sole purpose of hitting the tree again. A small buck might look over his shoulder to see if "anyone" is looking, but he will still rub a previously rubbed tree. My point is, the more times a tree is rubbed, the more damaged it appears. The rub becomes wider and longer with each rub, but it does not necessarily become deeply gouged. I sincerely believe that those trees with deep gouges are made by bucks with big antlers. Another indication of a big buck's presence are the limbs above and around the rubbed tree. Heavy broken and rubbed limbs, perhaps those with a one-inch diameter or more, tell me that a buck with massive antlers was responsible for the damage.

Now let's get back to rub lines. I sometimes hunt trails and food sources in early season where rubs are visible from my ambush location. Although I enjoy admiring them, they are no big deal because I know they are only sporadic rubs. However, a series of connecting rubs that extend for a certain distance through an area is considered a rub line—proof of a buck's existence and travel route.

In order to hunt a rub line successfully, you must be able to identify it positively as a rub line. The look of the trail along the rub line doesn't mean a thing. It does not have to be riddled with tracks or even noticeable to provide a hunting opportunity. Oftentimes, I can stand at one rub and see another a short distance away. Some are only twenty, thirty, or forty yards apart. Other times, I find it necessary to walk a short distance to find a connecting rub. The total distance of a rub line can vary, and two rubs could be fifty yards or more apart. I've seen some that were identifiable for only one hundred yards. The longest distance I have followed a rub line is about a quarter of a mile. Keep in mind, though, the rub line is the proof you need that a mature buck has traveled a given area more than once, and you don't always need a long rub line to ambush him. The pre-rut period is when a buck commits himself to following certain routes consistently, and the rub line he leaves behind lets you know where he might soon be.

Exactly where you will find a rub line could vary, but some areas seem to attract more bucks than others. First, consider that the densest areas usually provide the best locations for mature bucks to travel. Big bucks don't have a problem finding a thick area and making a rub line before the foliage vanishes in autumn.

I commonly find rub lines along fencelines. It's also true that many funnels and corridors force bucks to travel a specific zone. We've heard a lot about hunting funnels and bottlenecks, and rightfully so. However, not all of these routes are guaranteed to produce a rub line, nor do they provide proof of a big buck's existence.

Typically, a rub line is found somewhere between the buck's bedding area and food source, or bedding areas and food sources. A few years ago, during the early-archery season, I discovered such a rub line located in a heavily wooded area with a stand of oaks that were dropping acorns furiously. I considered it unlikely the buck that left the rubs would arrive at the food source in daylight hours, so I set up

The author took this huge eleven-pointer during the pre-rut period after setting up a stand along a rub line. *Photo by Vikki L. Trout*

a tree stand along the rub line about one hundred yards from the food source and what I assumed to be about two hundred yards from the bedding area. On my second hunt, a huge eleven-pointer walking the rub line offered a shooting opportunity, and today that buck hangs on my living-room wall. He grossed just over 140 inches and carried a double brow tine. Not my best buck, but the largest one I have taken along a rub line—a constant reminder of how productive this tactic can be.

The biggest mistake hunters make when searching for a rub line is letting a big buck know they are around. Following a rub line too far is a sure way of pushing a buck out of hiding. If this happens, you could spend countless hours waiting in ambush along a rub line that is already dead. For this reason, avoid following rubs too far and never follow them into a potential bedding area. I would also suggest you wear knee-high rubber boots to avoid leaving scent while following a rub line.

As mentioned previously, don't be surprised if no visible trail exists along a rub line. Consider the rub line itself as the trail, and set up as close to it as possible for the best chance of ambushing a buck.

Pre-rut rub lines are subject to recurrence. I've often discovered a rub line one year, only to find another in the same area or within close proximity the next year. I look for scarred trees when scouting so that I can pattern them and check them later to see if a buck has reopened the rub line. However, another factor to consider is that a rub line is more visible after the foliage decreases, so you should continue looking for rub lines throughout the pre-rut period. You could miss an active rub line one week but notice it the next simply because less foliage obscures the trees. One final suggestion: Always walk a given area thoroughly. Sometimes you won't notice a rub line until you have passed it coming and going.

One strong indication of a productive rub line is the freshness of the rubs, and experience is your best teacher. The more rubs you examine, the easier it becomes to tell a fresh rub from one that is ten days old. By the way, I consider a fresh rub one that was made within the past week. Bark shavings under a rubbed tree might provide some proof of freshness if leaves are falling; they will be on top of the fallen leaves and not covered. Just remember, bark shavings can last for eons if nothing disturbs them.

In ending this chapter, I should remind you about the home range of a buck during the pre-rut period. He travels daily in this area, and he will be consistent about leaving rubs along his travel routes. During the primary rut when a buck is covering ground, he will rub trees, sometimes vigorously, but that isn't proof he will return. The pre-rut rub line, however, tells you where he was, that he likes traveling this route and he has done it more than once.

I don't necessarily head for the woods in pre-rut seeking a rub line, hoping to find a big buck. On the contrary, I look for all sign and decide which will offer the best possibility to intercept a mature buck. If a rub line is what I find and it appears to offer the best potential, you can bet that I will select an ambush site nearby. Then again, there are times when neither rub lines nor even hot food sources offer the best possibilities for pre-rut success. Sometimes it's finding just one certain trail that will put me onto the right buck. ◼

6

Autumn Buck Trails

Wouldn't it be nice if any given area had only one primary trail? A hunter could simply set up along that trail and wait for the right buck. Enough said. Let's get back to reality. In most any area, several trails exist, and we know that the deer may use any of them, bypassing the trail we are watching. We know, too, that many deer walk other trails near our stands without ever stepping into a perfect shooting lane.

Like many hunters, my time used to be spent waiting near major runways, hoping a buck would go by. The possibility existed and sometimes it did happen. I assume that after so many efforts, the laws of average treated me fairly.

I soon realized though, that the hottest looking deer trails were not necessarily the best places to spend my time. It has always been human nature to hunt where we see the most deer sign, even when we hunt trophy bucks. We find an obvious trail carved deeply into the ground between the bedding and feeding areas. We follow it, spot a couple of rubs or maybe a scrape or two, and we become instantly attracted to the area.

MASTER VS. SECONDARY TRAILS

I refer to these runways as the "master trails." All deer use them occasionally, but just because they are the major highways of the deer woods, don't think for a moment that they will attract trophy bucks. You can often follow them easily for considerable distances, sometimes covering a mile or more, depending on food sources, bedding areas and terrain. They have been there for eons and they always remain visible. But their attraction lies more in their obvious appearance than in their effectiveness during the pre-rut period.

In a vast area, a master trail could run for miles; in farm country, it may only go a few hundred yards. Regardless of its length, a master trail is always an old route deer rely on for short distances to get from point A to point B.

Even though the trail is highly visible, you'll seldom find numerous droppings and tracks along the route. When you walk the master trails, though, without fail, you will notice other connecting smaller trails, which I'll refer to as "secondary trails."

Master trails are usually the oldest in the area and may be found year after year. However, these trails are more attractive to young bucks than mature ones.

They do not look anything like the master trails. In fact, instead of being an obvious wide and flattened deer highways, they are just the opposite, usually narrower and somewhat overgrown. But many of them are frequently used by bucks, and for good reason.

Naturally, bucks don't travel all secondary trails, but I believe that any of them are preferred by the bucks over master trails. When bucks travel master trails, they do so briefly. They might even follow a secondary trail to where it connects to a master trail, then follow the master trail for a short distance before picking up another secondary trail.

You probably already know that deer seldom travel right on a trail; they tend to stray on and off, but always going in the direction of the trail. The point is, all deer rely on a trail to guide them.

No matter where I hunt, I've always observed that mature bucks like it thick. Since some secondary trails lead to thick areas, and a buck might pass by any time, I try to study the system carefully so I can practically count on action.

LOCATING THE RIGHT TRAILS

During the earliest part of the pre-rut period, I find and walk the master trails to help me easily locate the secondary trails, any of which could be an outstanding route for bucks. Although the scraping period and the primary rut are several weeks away, the rubbing has already begun. If a buck or two are using the secondary trail, you can bet that there will be rubs and often an obvious rub line.

In the previous chapter I discussed both rub lines and sporadic rubs. For just a moment, let me say something about sporadic rubs that wasn't mentioned before. I have frequently discovered nests of sporadic rubs at the exact spot where a secondary trail links to the master trail. I don't really know why this occurs. But I do know it indicates a buck has used the secondary trail. Thus, I watch these sporadic rubs and use them as evidence—a reason to follow the secondary trail. This often leads to a rub line.

I would not suggest you follow a secondary trail too far. I like to know where it leads, but keep in mind the secondary trails do not generally cover a major distance. They can lead to bedding and feeding areas or they may just be a connecting trail that leads to the master trail.

I back off whenever I notice the trail begins to lead into extremely dense cover. I assume this could be a bedding area and the last thing I want to do is let a mature buck know I'm around.

On the other hand, if the the evidence leads from one master trail to another,

Secondary trails that lead into thick cover and possible bedding areas could be the most active buck travel routes in the area.

and there is no bedding area between, I assume it is simply a connecting runway. I seldom find such trails to be laced with rubs and I usually avoid them. I have also followed secondary trails to oak thickets and other secluded foods—often reliable buck trails to hunt. But those secondary trails that link to a dense and possible bedding area have always provided me with the best possibility of ambushing a trophy whitetail.

UNBEATABLE FORCED BUCK ROUTES

When I climbed into my stand during the Illinois firearm season two years before writing this book, two factors were against me. Unseasonably warm temperatures had slowed deer movement for the past few days, and a preliminary report indicated a sharp decline in the overall harvest. Nonetheless, a buck trail near a fenceline fifty yards to the west had become a forced travel zone for bucks in the area; more about why I could count on that fenceline in just a moment.

When I heard the rustling of leaves, I fully expected to see a gray squirrel busily doing his thing. Surprisingly though, I saw glistening white antlers bobbing up and down as the buck took each step. A moment after the initial shock of spotting him had passed, I shouldered my slugster. A few rapid heartbeats later, my crosshairs found the target.

As I approached the 140-inch Boone and Crockett eight-pointer, I could see he had fallen on the trail that ran parallel to the fence a few steps away. Then I recalled another big buck I had missed near the same fenceline during the earlier archery

After setting up a stand along a fenceline, the author took this 140-inch, eight-point buck. *Photo by Vikki L. Trout.*

season. To look at the trail, though, you would never believe it was a hot route. In fact, the sign along the fence was not laced in tracks and droppings. However, this travel route did what few others do. It forced the action.

I enjoy studying trails, and always keep an eye open for interesting buck sign. Most trails that I encounter are simply options to a traveling buck. He may use this one, or he may use that one. On the other hand, there are trails that bucks will use more often than others. You could say they prefer these trails or, at least, you could say they are forced to use them. Be aware that the forced travel routes I speak of are a small percentage of existing secondary trails.

Hunters often prefer to hunt trails where there is plenty of visibility. But sometimes trails in the least visible areas will attract the mature bucks.

Naturally, hunters sometimes kill bucks along master trails. I have hunted them and have occasionally enjoyed success. However, I would bet that a buck using a master trail during the day is simply taking a shortcut to a forced travel zone. In fact, he will probably travel the master trail only as far as it takes to reach the forced route. So the real reason for hunting the secondary, forced route is because you narrow down the field.

In most areas, you can assume there aren't many forced travel routes. When searching for such areas, take a systematical, logical approach and look for anything that might make a deer move in a given direction.

Although deer can easily jump a five-foot fence, even a lower one will force them to walk along it for a given distance. Such was the case where I shot the big buck just mentioned. A doe had walked on almost the same path twenty minutes before I saw the buck. Along the fence you could see a trail, but not as distinct as the master trail one hundred yards in the opposite direction, which crossed through the middle of a huge and open hardwoods.

Actually, I had originally set up along the master trail in the vast hardwoods. I saw several deer, but most were a considerable distance off and not using the trail I watched. That's the common scenario when hunting the master trails. Nevertheless, I did see several bucks along the fenceline. I also knew that unless

I made a move, I would eventually spot a good buck farther away than desired. When I did move, I placed my stand about fifty yards from the fence. The buck I shot was within spitting distance of the fence.

There's more to hunting fencelines than just waiting in ambush along one, however. All fencelines are straight, which means the trails along them are straight as well. The fenceline I hunted covered more than four hundred yards from north to south. In addition, like most preferred travel routes along fences, there was cover on both sides of the fence.

Once the deer hit this fenceline, they would usually follow it to a corner where it bumped into another fence that ran from east to west. I might add, my stand was only about seventy yards from the corner. Thus, regardless of which fence a buck traveled, the possibility was good for him to be within easy range of my firearm.

The real asset of the fencelines I hunted, and most others for that matter, was the opening in one of the fences near the corner of the two. At the opening, the fence was bent over and only half as tall as the rest of the fence. Most of the deer

that traveled these two fencelines would head directly for this corner and the opening. They could jump either of the fences any-where, and would do so if neces-sary (my wife bumped into a buck and doe one evening and sent them leaping over at that location), but most will head for the easiest crossing.

If you do locate a fence in your area, look for attractive crossing points. If barbed wire is present, you might find hair on the fence, indicating that deer frequently cross at that location. The point is, there will be a limit-ed number of fence crossings. Once you find these, you have found the best trail to ambush the right buck.

If a fenceline is not available, look for other areas that have become forced travel zones. A funnel that derives from a large

Funnels are natural travel routes. However, those that connect to bottlenecks and other funnels might offer the best oppor-tunities for a filling tag. *Photo by Vicki L. Trout.*

Hot secondary trails are often found along creeks and ditches. A mature buck buck might consistently cross at one location.

body of timber or thickets, but empties into an open field on the other end, seldom becomes a buck trail. Even if you find an obvious trail through the funnel, don't count on a mature buck being there during daylight hours. On the other hand, if a funnel is met on both ends with additional funnels, you have found a forced travel corridor and a possible hot buck trail. In many farmlands, these types of funnels are not difficult to locate. You only need to make certain that you set up at the point where one funnel connects with another, and you can effectively cover two funnels instead of one. Obviously, you should select the connection where the wind is favorable.

A bottleneck is an area where a narrow funnel suddenly widens. It's possible and even better, however, to locate a funnel with two bottle-necks—one on each end. Again, though, you should plan your ambush close to one of the connections, or bottlenecks. If only one bottleneck exists, select an ambush location where it forms, and hunt it only when a favorable wind exists. If you have two bottlenecks, the odds shift in your favor because you can hunt the one where the wind is favorable.

Of course, it's possible that you won't find any fencelines, funnels, and bottlenecks in your area—which does not mean forced travel zones do not exist. On the contrary, natural terrain that has not been interrupted by man's clearing might still host unbeatable buck routes.

Ditches, creeks, and ravines are similar to fencelines. They are seldom straight, but they still force deer to travel certain routes. Like fences, the best travel routes along them are close to the crossings. Once a buck establishes a preferred crossing point at these natural landmarks, he will use it consistently.

Perhaps the most difficult task of all is locating the unbeatable travel routes. You can spend countless hours walking and searching for such trails, and still fail to locate those that offer the most potential. I've found that the best way to locate funnels, bottlenecks, fencelines, and natural forced travel zones is to view topographic maps and aerial photos. The Internet has made this easier than ever before. You can search for maps of your area at *www.terraserver.com* or *www.mytopo.com.*

ESCAPE BUCK TRAILS

There's another kind of buck trail worth hunting, particularly late in the pre-rut period, when the pressure intensifies. Forget about the hot buck trails you hunted earlier and look for escape trails—those that lead to places where the bucks are hiding.

Understanding a buck's habits when hunting pressure increases is the best way to locate escape trails. First, don't always assume that bucks will become totally nocturnal. It may appear that they have, but you can bet that the first thirty minutes after dawn breaks and the last thirty minutes before dusk are prime times to intercept a wary mature buck—provided you are hunting the trail close to his hideout.

Any thick location of honeysuckle and bramble bushes or cutover areas may contain escape trails used by bucks, and even grown-up fields—areas where

Whitetails usually cross fences at a location that is most attractive. Oftentimes, if barbed wire is present, hair will be found at a preferred crossing.

few people venture—become attractive to them. I'll be discussing buck hideouts thoroughly in a later chapter, but I mention them now just to let you know that most secondary trails that offer potential for ambushing a mature buck exist early in the pre-rut period. When the heat is on, buck trails are commonly found in escape areas.

Escape trails can be difficult to locate because they do not show up as readily as master and secondary trails; you may not locate a distinct trail at all—only tracks. A buck may or may not use an area consistently, and the amount of sign you find will depend on how often he has been there. Tracks, though, are the bulk of the sign. Rubs are not as common along an escape trail as they are a secondary trail earlier in pre-rut.

Before moving on, I want to point out that I'm not so sure that a true buck trail—one used exclusively by bucks—really exists in any area. However, keep in mind that a hot buck trail is any trail that attracts a buck on the day you are there.

MOCK TRAVEL ROUTES

Most hunters have heard of mock scrapes and how they can increase hunting opportunities, but few of us have considered creating mock trails. I became excited about this routine a few years ago after clearing a walking path to my stand. I wanted to avoid leaving my scent on brush and nearby deer trails and to allow a quiet, simple approach. A short time later, though, I discovered the deer had also begun using my trail. In fact, I soon became dependent upon this manmade trail for producing action. Clearly, the same technique could work elsewhere.

Even bucks like traveling the easy routes to get to their destinations. They don't enjoy difficult maneuvering, and will not go out of their way unless forced. However, all this can change when you install a mock travel route.

While you should scout and locate the better secondary buck

A mock trail might attract the right buck. However, the less clearing you have to do to create a trail, the better your chances are that a buck will use it.

trails mentioned previously, it is also true that you can make good things happen, regardless of the trail you hunt. Not every hunting situation calls for a mock trail, but when the need arises, a little work could turn your luck around.

Always consider the surrounding area. In hilly country, place mock trails along hillsides. Deer seldom travel straight up—or down—but prefer to move along trails that move horizontally, or along a hill. The trail may go up, but it does so gradually. When hunting narrow hollows, preferred trails usually cross them. Deer are unlikely to travel a valley from one end to the other.

Some cutover areas attract whitetails because the new growth provides food, while the dense vegetation provides them with a secure bedding zone. However, deer cannot maneuver freely in areas with too many thick log jams. Here's the bottom line: You should set up a mock trail in the whitetail's preferred area by locating natural secondary travel routes and customizing them to suit your needs, or construct an entirely new trail where passage has been nearly impossible.

The less clearing you have to do to create a trail, the better the chance that deer will use it. I have seen many deer balk when walking into areas that were cleared too well.

If a buck uses the secondary trail you have located but fails to offer a shooting

Even though mature bucks prefer traveling routes in dense areas, they do not like to travel through areas they cannot easily maneuver.

opportunity, reroute him by moving natural fallen debris onto an existing travel route. Strategically placed, the debris should push the deer towards you if an open pathway exists. If not, remove limbs and debris to clear the way for deer to move toward your stand.

ENHANCING FUNNELS AND BOTTLENECKS

Funnels and bottlenecks probably offer some of the best buck trails, and the best places to set up mock trails. These natural travel corridors attract bucks anyway, and seldom does it take more than a minor adjustment to put a big one where you want him.

When a mock trail is necessary in a funnel or bottleneck, I place it at the narrowest location, do the necessary clearing and use obstructions to push the deer toward me. If a fenceline or creek exists and you locate a crossing point where you cannot locate your stand, try blocking the crossing point to force the deer to cross the fence or ditch where you can set up.

Consider one last thing before constructing a mock trail: Always be aware of laws that may not allow cutting on public land, and always tell the landowner what you intend to do when hunting private land.

Finding deer trails and waiting in ambush nearby is nothing new. Many of us rely on this traditional hunting method each season. However, you could say that some trails have it while others don't. So why do certain trails attract mature bucks while others only waste your time? The season, the type of trail you locate and its purpose will provide the answer.

Throughout this first section, I have discussed various methods for intercepting trophy whitetails during the pre-rut period. Each is an effective tactic, but we all know that even a sure-fire technique can go terribly wrong. Fortunately, you have other options when the interception tactics don't work. ▪

7

Luring 'Em In

fter seeing the title of this chapter, you might assume that the next few pages will give all the facts about various ways to lure in bucks—from calls to decoys and scents. However, since this book is based upon advanced strategies, this chapter will not provide "general and typical" techniques common to those found in many other deer-hunting books. On the contrary, your tactics should differ from one stage of the rut to the other.

For instance, during the pre-rut period, grunt calls will work. However, when it comes to luring in mature bucks, save the grunting techniques for the primary rut, when they work best. The same theory applies to decoys and scents, which are most likely to fool big bucks once the breeding begins.

If you're thinking there can't be much left to discuss in the way of pre-rut lure tactics, you're right. Nevertheless, there are two strategies still on the back burner. Both antler rattling and bleat calls are quite effective tools when used properly during a certain time frame before the primary rut.

BUCK BATTLES

Before getting into rattling techniques, you should have some understanding of bucks that engage in battle, and why that conflict might or might not attract other bucks. There are two types of battles: 1) Sparring matches. 2) Knock-down, drag-out fights. Both occur during the pre-rut period, but sparring matches are ten times more common than major fights.

All bucks participate in sparring to condition neck muscles, and sometimes to establish hierarchy. Many biologists feel this is the primary reason for such occurrences, and there is probably some truth to the theory. Nevertheless, I'm not so sure that other factors don't contribute as much or more. When it comes to bucks, I believe sparring is as much a social behavioral action as anything else. However, even when friendly sparring occurs, it can lead to the No. 2 knock-down. In other words, in the animal kingdom, one male is always ready to take out another if opportunity allows.

While photographing sparring matches amongst whitetails, I've often observed friendly sparring matches that suddenly turned vicious when one became hurt. Sometimes it occurred when the loser was poked in the wrong place and then attempted to get away. The winning buck would forget about the "no hitting below the belt" rule, and take full advantage of the situation to let his opponent have it.

On one occasion, I remember watching two immature bucks spar off and on for more than an hour—a friendly match all the way. The two were never aggressive. At one point right in the middle of the sparring match, they both stopped and groomed each other for a brief period. Nevertheless, when one of the bucks suddenly lost his footing along the side of a ditch and nearly fell to the ground, the other seemed to become ravaging mad, pushing his antlers violently and rapidly into the other. No doubt, he could have cared less that it was his buddy he was trying to kill. When the buck on the bottom finally got to his feet, he ran away for parts unknown.

I said all this to let you know that it does not necessarily require a mature and dominant deer to turn a sparring match into a near deadly battle in a heartbeat. Any buck will become dominant the moment it knows it can win.

One-and-a-half year-old bucks do most of the sparring, but mature bucks do so occasionally. Matches begin when one buck provides an opportunity by lowering his head. The other buck will almost always accept the challenge, even when antler sizes vary, although I have never seen bucks with large antlers spar with young bucks.

When the sparring begins, the antlers of one buck slowly touch the antlers of the other. No real force is exerted, yet. The sounds are light and there is little or no shoving. Most sparring matches end without a winner and a loser, unless one has the opportunity to take advantage of another, as mentioned previously.

WHEN TO RATTLE

Timing is of the essence when rattling antlers to attract a mature buck. Doing it too early in autumn is often wasted effort. In fact, rattling at the wrong time might even send a signal to a buck that something is not on the up-and-up.

Sparring begins right after bucks lose their velvet. The beginning is slow, and even as the sparring intensifies with each passing week, it does not become frequent until about two to three weeks before the rut peaks. The best window of opportunity for rattling occurs about ten days before the rut peaks (the day breeding begins). As the pre-rut period progresses, sparring matches intensify. Serious battles are more likely, which sets the stage for a buck to walk in and investigate the source of the fight he hears. However, keep in mind we're talking about rattling in mature bucks. Sparring can lure in young bucks anytime during pre-rut, but trophy whitetails seldom respond to rattling until they know there is a good reason for the fight.

As the breeding draws near, the possibility exists that two bucks will engage in a battle over a nearby doe. Granted, I've witnessed many young bucks begin to spar

Rattling antlers and getting the attention of a mature buck is more likely during the two weeks to ten days prior to the primary rut. Young bucks typically respond to rattling earlier during pre-rut than do mature bucks.

when they walk into a field where a doe is already present. The doe just seems to trigger the sparring match. The big boys, though, don't take the rattling antlers seriously until they know the breeding is about to become serious. *That's* when the hunter should rattle seriously.

THE RIGHT ANTLERS

I own several sets of rattling antlers—more than I'll ever need—and they all have one thing in common: They are not large, massive antlers. In fact, most are small and spindly.

The antlers do not have to be matched, nor do they need lots of points to attract a mature buck. I prefer sets with at least six points and sets with eight points are ideal. Too many points are rough on your hands and make it more difficult to get the right sounds; too few points don't produce the right sounds either.

Although you can sometimes locate perfect rattling antlers when searching for sheds, you can also purchase synthetic antlers. Some of them sound fabulous, others sound terrible. Most companies that manufacture synthetic antlers offer added features. They can be darkened and camouflaged, making them safer to pack around and reducing the chance they will be spotted by an approaching whitetail when in use.

Most companies also keep the tips of the points blunt to prevent injury to the hunter. Naturally, sharp points are rougher on your hands, which is exactly why many individuals cut the tips off actual antlers. Personally, I prefer little or nothing cut off the points. One-half to one full inch isn't bad, but cutting too much causes the antlers to sound dead. Higher frequency sounds, such as those produced by tinkling the ends of the points together, seem to work best when luring a buck in close. Always tinkle real antlers together to get an idea of what sounds good. Then you can compare them to synthetic antlers and find out how they stand up to the real thing.

Many companies also offer rattling devices in a bag. These synthetic rattlers sound much better than some synthetic antlers, and they are much easier to store away than the real thing. The only thing they can't do, however, is create the sounds of a knock-down drag-out fight.

ANTLER RATTLING TECHNIQUES

In my opinion, there are two times to rattle antlers. One occurs when you see a passing buck that will not come to within range. The other is when the buck's antlers are obscured because he is too far off or too deep in cover. In either case, rattling might get him to stop or come to you.

I have found that bucks respond to rattling better in the morning, but do not restrict your rattling to mornings only.

Consider my hunt to the Alberta, Canada, Bow Zone in 1990. I had done some rattling back in the Midwest and although I had seen a few bucks come in, I had never witnessed a mature buck respond to rattling. My outfitter, Jim Hole, Jr., had asked me to use rattling horns occasionally, as he had enjoyed success on many occasions.

The timing was certainly right, since the peak-rut was about two weeks away when I arrived. About three days into my hunt, my rattling brought in a respectable eight-pointer. I passed the good buck at fifteen yards, hoping to cash in on a better one before the week ended. I saw small bucks sparring in fields, and even spotted a couple of other wall hangers on the move as the week progressed. However, sour weather prevailed, and by the time the last evening rolled around, it looked like I would return to Indiana without a huge Alberta buck.

Shortly after climbing into my stand that evening, the wind began to shift and blow my scent into the woods, right where the deer should come from. Not long after, I heard a deer blowing repeatedly. Since the deer had obviously discovered my ambush location, I climbed down and walked to a spot where the wind was favorable. I stood behind a clump of maples ten yards from the edge of the field, and within bow range of a nearby trail leading to it. I had about ninety minutes of hunting time before dusk.

Light rain, a gusty wind, and cold temperatures made the time pass slowly.

Although I was somewhat saddened my hunt would soon be over, it almost seemed delightful to know that I was finally only thirty minutes away from getting out of the nasty elements of the Alberta Bow Zone.

Not one to quit without a final game plan, I decided to rattle antlers as the light faded. The first two sessions (each lasted a couple of minutes) produced nothing. As I finished the third and last session, though, I spotted movement to my left along the edge of the field no more than thirty yards away. My first thought: a coyote was on the prowl. I had seen more of them than deer. But within seconds, I realized I was seeing the body of a deer, and, I spotted huge headgear almost as quickly. My arm was already nervously reaching for my bow that had hung on a limb.

It took only about one minute for a shooting opportunity to arrive. The buck had stopped and stood broadside twenty yards from me. Then his head turned as he scanned the woods to look for the bucks that he had heard fighting. I took advantage of the moment and drew my bowstring. A moment later, I heard the thump of the arrow as it hit home.

The buck now hangs on my living room wall and continues to provide the encouragement I need for future rattling episodes. His twelve points provided a Pope and Young gross score of 158 inches.

So the two best times to rattle are when you see a buck—and when you don't. Always tinkle the points together after you spot a buck that needs to come closer. Never start by sounding like a fight. However, if the buck doesn't stop, don't be afraid to increase the tempo. Odds are he didn't hear the tinkling of the antlers, but any buck will at least stop if he hears the rattling. Once he does, give him another low-volume tinkling session to let him identify the location. No other rattling is necessary. He will either come, or he won't. If he doesn't, and you are sure he's heard the rattling, you will only arouse his suspicion by continuing.

Most hunters who rattle antlers do so in hopes that the right buck will hear it. These bucks often appear out of nowhere, such as the Alberta buck I discussed. Unfortunately, some hunters rattle too much, or not enough.

Never go to your ambush location with the idea of rattling off-and-on for two or three hours. You will only waste your time and spoil it for another day. On the other hand, some hunters will rattle once and give up after nothing shows. A loss of confidence is probably the biggest reason why rattling fails. Many hunters don't try rattling more than once per season simply because a buck didn't come in running the first time.

When rattling, begin gently in case a buck is close. I start easy but don't mind increasing the tempo when that fails to attract a customer. Some hunters say you should never simulate a hard-nosed battle. I disagree. The sounds of a major battle carry farther than tinkled sparring sounds, and are more likely to attract a mature buck. On the other hand, if you're hoping to attract an immature buck, you might want to stick to a low-volume sparring match.

In the mornings, I start rattling about thirty minutes after dawn. I rattle lightly for about two or three minutes and watch enthusiastically for another two or three minutes. If nothing shows, I increase the volume and make the fight sound more serious for two or three minutes. I wait again and try rattling one more time. I hang the antlers out of harm's way and don't rattle any more for at least another hour. Then I will often repeat the process one more time.

When I arrive on stand late in the afternoon, I rely upon my ambush location to produce the action. I begin rattling about forty-five minutes

Many hunters lose confidence and never try rattling again if they don't get action the first time. The author recommends rattling only during the pre-rut, when you have the best chance to lure a buck in close.

before dusk and try three rattling sessions again. They take about fifteen minutes or less to complete. Once it's over, I hang up the antlers for the remainder of the evening and rely again on the ambush location. Some bucks simply will not appear until the light of day is nearly gone, even though they probably heard the rattling antlers sometime earlier.

BUCK-TO-DOE RATIOS

You should understand that rattling success is dependent upon the area, and the wrong buck-to-doe ratio will severely reduce your chances of luring a buck into range. You should also understand that the number of does to each buck varies considerably from one area to another. Every state or province has some spots where there are several does to every buck; you need to concentrate on those that have the least number of does.

I believe it boils down to competition. Consider the late 1980s in southern Indiana, where EHD (Epizootic Hemorrhagic Disease) struck a few counties hard. EHD usually kills more does and fawns than antlered bucks, and many had been

The buck-to-doe ratio has much to do with rattling in bucks. The fewer does per buck, the better rattling works.

obliterated by the disease in late summer and early fall (myself and others discovered sixteen carcasses during a few weeks). But although we saw very few does when hunting, bucks were spotted much more than usual, probably because they moved more in search of does. My point is that rattling is best in areas where breeding is the most competitive.

The ideal ratio for rattling success is probably two or three does to each buck. That doesn't necessarily mean you won't experience action where there are six or seven bucks to each doe. I've seen rattling work in such situations. It's just that you can expect business to be a little slow when there are numerous does.

UNDERSTANDING BLEATS

I'll discuss deer calling and primarily grunt calls in depth in a later chapter. However, doe bleats will often lure a buck in during the pre-rut period.

All deer bleat. It is standard social talk amongst them, used by does, bucks, and fawns more often than any other sound. But you already know that deer are not vocal animals, and they don't walk around bleating all the time. They will bleat when under severe stress, but casual bleating occurs even when all is well. For instance, a doe looking for her fawn might bleat consistently for hours. A fawn, even a six-month-old one, might bleat all day in search of its mother. During the rut, when bucks chase does away from fawns, the fawns will sometimes walk around and bleat. Then again, an adult buck or doe might bleat for no apparent reason as it approaches another deer, or just walks a trail.

I've heard far more deer bleat while photographing them and while studying captive deer than I have while hunting , and I've noticed that there is little difference in the sounds of adult deer. The bleat of a buck is much like that of a doe. Fawns, on the other hand, have a higher pitched bleat, and does that are searching for fawns produce a lower-sounding bleat than when they are just socializing with other deer.

Several companies manufacture bleat calls, and some incorporate grunts, allowing you to make several different sounds with one call. Personally, I don't like the idea of rotating a dial or doing something else to switch from a grunt or bleat call. I say this because when a buck is around (the only time I use a call), the last thing I want is to have to concentrate on something other than the buck.

Bleat calls are often effective, but I sometimes use my voice. If my throat is clear, I can produce great sounding bleats that require no movement, and many other hunters can do the same. It doesn't require a certain kind of voice. When my son was only twelve-years-old, he attracted the first antlered buck he ever tagged by bleating to him.

Bleats are simply a "baaaah." They are short and crisp. Each baaaah should last about one second or slightly more. Never drag them on for two or three seconds, and never force the sound into syllables. A long "baa-aaa-aaa-aaa-aaah" is how sheep bleat.

BLEATING TACTICS

Unlike rattling, which I prefer to do sporadically in hopes a customer will hear it, I save the pre-rut bleats for when I know a customer is there. Sitting around in a tree stand and bleating every few minutes is not recommended unless you really want to put a curse on your hunting area. However, during the pre-rut period, particularly the two or three weeks before the primary rut, a bleat to a passing buck can turn an unfavorable situation into a moment of great happiness in less than a heartbeat.

A bleat, coupled with thick foliage, will sometimes force a buck to hunt for you. Even a firearm hunter can appreciate that, but when bowhunting, this is exactly what you hope for when calling to a buck.

I would suggest, though, you never call to a buck that is downwind. He will stop as you wish, but he will promptly scent you. Then it's over for that day and possibly many more. Had you not called, this buck might have walked by you without ever knowing you were there. That's a much better ending.

Deer do not bleat loudly. However, you should make certain a passing buck will hear you when you call. I've often heard hunters say that a buck didn't pay

Save the bleat call until you see a buck pass by out of range. Then use the call to get his attention.

attention to them, when it's highly likely the buck just never heard the call. If I bleat once and a buck doesn't stop, I do it again—louder. If that doesn't make him stop, I increase the volume again. When I'm sure he heard the call, I bleat once more so he knows where it came from. Don't wait too long to come back with a second bleat, however. Some bucks will stop and start walking away again just a second or two after hearing the first bleat.

If you use a commercial bleat call, make certain it is not a fawn bleat. I've heard a couple of supposedly doe bleat calls that sounded more like fawn bleats. The high-volume sounds may arouse a doe's curiosity, but fawn bleats will seldom bring a mature buck into range.

Bleat calls and rattling antlers should not become relied upon tactics. Instead, think of them as tools to use during pre-rut only when other strategies fail. Look at it this way: You are the predator, and it's more advantageous for a predator to make it a guessing game. You can't do that by calling and rattling too much, so focus on never giving away your position. ▪

8

Keep Them Guessing

No matter how well you sharpen the pre-rut hunting tactics mentioned in this book, any will fail if you can't keep the bucks guessing. In other words, you might have discovered the perfect ambush location near a hot, secluded food source. Perhaps you found a rub line that is out of this world. Maybe the fence-line trail you stumbled across leads directly to a big buck's hideout. Any of these discoveries make it possible for you to ambush an unsuspecting buck. Notice, I said "unsuspecting." The odds are never in favor of the hunter, but they are unbelievably against you if you arouse suspicion, and when hunting a mature buck, you arouse suspicion if you let him know you are there. It often takes only one little thing going wrong to waste your time and money.

Before proceeding, allow me to point out (again) that we are still discussing pre-rut whitetails. During the primary rut, bucks are moving consistently and taking all kinds of chances. They really don't get much of an opportunity to detect your presence, and you don't get the opportunity to keep them guessing, because most

During the pre-rut period, before bucks are on the move in search of does, you must take the necessary precautions to keep him guessing.

bucks don't stay in one place long enough. As I've already said in this book, it takes a whole lot more expertise to hunt for, then pattern and ambush a mature buck during pre-rut. During the primary rut, you can climb a tree on the fringes of St. Louis and possibly see a buck crossing a highway and dodging vehicles while he searches for does. You could even get lucky and kill the buck, but you won't get a chance to pattern him and make mistakes trying to.

There are several ways to keep a buck guessing, and the first consideration is probably human scent. I am not talking about setting up your ambush location so that you are not downwind of an approaching buck. Nope. You know the common-sense stuff already. This book is about advanced strategies.

GETTING IN AND OUT

Well-known and successful bowhunter Myles Keller once told me that he wished he could drop out of the sky to get into his tree stand. I love that statement. It is so true, and Keller should know. He's taken several Pope and Young whitetails, and he's been around the country block enough times to know that getting in and out of the area is how many hunters warn a mature buck of their presence—sometimes before the hunting gets started.

I've never forgotten early October of 1997. I walked into the woods and dropped my stand so that I could move it only forty yards—closer to a white oak that was dropping acorns by the pound every minute. As I walked toward the oak, my leg brushed against a small maple tree no more than three feet tall. I hated it, but I thought surely it could not possibly get me into trouble.

Later that evening, as I sat back enjoying a delightful fading sunset, I spotted movement in the thickets bordering the hardwoods. Then I saw huge antlers. The beams were a dark walnut color, extremely heavy and tall. When the buck stood facing into me no more than sixty yards away, I knew he would probably score 160-plus inches.

When the buck started walking toward me, his head was only about a foot off the ground. He was just twenty yards from being within bow range when he suddenly stopped, stretched his neck and scented the maple I had bumped against earlier. He remained motionless and stared ahead of him. Seconds later, he lowered his head and scented the maple again. Once more, he jerked his head away from my scent and stared ahead. This went on for five solid minutes, then he turned around and sneaked back into the brush from where he had come.

What happened that day has haunted me for years, and I can't help but think about how often it might have happened without me even knowing it. Keller's statement is right on target.

I'm sure you've heard about rubber boots, and how much less likely it is for them to leave human scent than leather boots. After hunting black bear and dealing

Knee-high rubber boots will allow you to get in and out of your area without leaving as much human scent behind as you would in leather boots. *Photo by Vikki L. Trout.*

with their perfect noses for more than twenty years, I know rubber boots are the best thing to put on your feet when hunting whitetails. I'm not so sure they are totally scent-free once a human foot has been inside them and sweated for hours, but I they are as close to perfect as you can get.

When scent does escape from rubber boots, it probably escapes through the openings at the top where you tuck in your pants. The best news is that seventeen-inch rubber boots go further up your leg than do nine-inch leather boots, allowing you to walk through taller weeds without leaving scent.

When walking to and from your stand, always avoid the overgrown areas. The higher the vegetation, the more scent you leave and disturbance you create. That's exactly why I don't have any problem with walking deer trails when wearing rubber boots. Of course, I avoid overhanging limbs, etc., since they can surely get me into trouble.

Taking the easy route is not necessarily the best route. For instance, it could be that when you go to your morning stand, all you need to do is walk across this one hundred-yard open field to get there. That's much easier than walking through a dark woods for three hundred yards. Yep, it's easier, but it sure isn't the right thing to do.

In the mornings, use common sense and walk through areas where deer are least likely to be. Since mature whitetail bucks are sometimes nocturnal, food sources are not included. When your morning hunt ends, you can walk the open field since the deer will likely be in, or close to the bedding area.

Plan your approach and departure wisely. Avoid walking through food plots at dawn and dusk and avoid walking close to bedding areas during the day, even if you must walk further to get in and out.

Apply the same philosophy for evening, but reverse the in-and-out rules. When leaving your ambush site, avoid the fields where deer are, or will soon be. Take the long route if necessary to avoid spooking the buck you hope to kill the next day. The rules are straightforward: In early morning and late evening, avoid food sources or getting too close to them. In late morning and early evening, avoid bedding areas or getting too close to them. Always take the long route if necessary to do so.

One final suggestion about getting in and out: Arrive early in the mornings and leave late in the evenings. The darker, the better. For example, if you hunt a food source in the evenings, be prepared to sit until dark if deer are around. You can't keep a buck guessing by leaving your ambush location when the alarm clock rings. On the other hand, if you hunt by a food source in the evening and there are no deer around when darkness is minutes away, take advantage of the situation and bail out. Sitting five more minutes is a good way to be stuck.

RAINY-DAY SCOUTING

If you hunt seriously for mature whitetail bucks (which is probably the case if you are reading this book), you know the importance of continuous scouting during pre-rut. Things change fast and you must always keep looking here and there to pattern a certain big buck.

I agree with hunters who claim you can overdo your scouting. Too much is one sure way to let a big buck know you are there. Your luck will run out and you will bump him, or you will create disturbance and leave scent behind. On the contrary, though, if you hunt for a trophy whitetail, you have to stay on top of things and continuous scouting is the only way to do it. You must take risks, but you have to be smart about it.

That's exactly why I love to do my looking on rainy days, or just before the rain arrives. Thanks to jobs and other obligations that interfere with our hunting, we don't get many chances to do so. However, every deer hunter should take advantage of the somber days whenever possible.

When scouting during a rain, you can move about quietly with little or no disturbance. Fresh sign is more difficult to find, but that you must forfeit. Some guys claim that scouting right after a rain provides the best opportunities to locate sign. They are somewhat correct, and I will discuss this in more detail in Section II. However, we're talking about pre-rut bucks before scrapes become a major issue. Scouting during the rain is absolutely the best thing you can do

Continuous scouting is important for patterning big bucks during the pre-rut period. To avoid letting the bucks know where you have been, do your scouting just before or during the rain. *Photo by Vikki L. Trout.*

during pre-rut. Keep in mind, when scouting during primary rut, the bucks are moving and don't get a chance to pattern you like they can during pre-rut. You're probably tired of hearing me say that, but it's one of those things that I can't help but keep mentioning.

The best news about scouting in the rain, or just before, is that scent might not be a problem. Nobody can say just how long your scent stays, since there's no feasible way to run a test, but when you scout several days before a rain, you can bet your scent will be around a long time. I'm sure humidity and wind also play a role in the lifespan of scent, and I don't like taking chances. Bloodhounds have picked up scent that is days old when favorable conditions exist. Who would doubt that a whitetail's nose might not be even better than that of a bloodhound?

Consider, too, that when you scout just after a rain, you will leave scent on every little wet piece of foliage you bump against. Have you ever smelled a wet dog? That gives you an idea of how moisture agitates scent. Scouting before or during rain lets you alleviate these problems.

STAY ON THE MOVE

Of all the ways you can keep a big buck guessing, nothing beats staying on the move. The more stands you have to choose from, the better your chance of intercepting Mr. Right.

I've always believed ambush sites are most productive the first few times you hunt them, and the first and second times are the best. The third and fourth are okay, but afterwards your chances decrease tremendously. After hunting an area several times, even when the wind is favorable, it will seem to dry up for obvious reasons.

Regardless of how careful you are, you'll leave some human scent near a stand each time you hunt. Then there is the scent distribution and disturbance factor we already discussed when getting in and out.

To keep the bucks guessing, consider selecting several ambush sites and stay on the move. This keeps you positioned where wind direction is always favorable. The more options you have, the more first- and second-time hunts you can enjoy.

When an area does drop dead, I've found that moving just one hundred yards is often all it takes to avoid educating a wise, mature buck. Of course,

Just how long human scent remains on debris is unknown. However, we do know that a whitetail's nose is one of the best in the animal kingdom.

The author has always believed that the first and second time you hunt a stand are the best. For this reason, remain versatile and select several ambush sites. The more you have to choose from, the more you can keep the bucks guessing. *Photo by Vikki L. Trout.*

hunters sometimes have difficulty moving away from certain ambush sites, simply because they saw the buck of their dreams. Forget the past and think of the future. You can't kill a buck that's already walked by you, but you can kill one that is about to show up.

Consider owning as many portable stands as you can afford. Climbing stands are not necessarily beneficial because they usually won't allow you to get in and out of the area as quietly. They do have their place, and will allow you to move from one area to the other at a moment's notice. Nevertheless, portable stands help you to stay versatile because they are there—ready and waiting for you.

BEATING THE WIND

As I said previously, this book is not about what should be common-sense, like hunting where the wind is favorable. Instead, I want to discuss ways you can beat the wind.

First, avoid hunting in holes. When your stand is surrounded by small hills or big ridges on two or more, disaster can strike quickly. All it takes is for a wind that is blowing perfectly one moment to start blowing from opposite direction the next moment. However, this scenario should not be confused with variable winds. In fact, the wind may be steady everywhere else except in the hole where your stand is set. When you are in a hole, the wind often bounces from one high point to another. A buck might appear, but you can bet your scent will pass in front of his nose before he gets to you.

When variable winds exist, select ambush sites near open areas. The wind direction will be more consistent, and there is less chance a buck will know you are there.

Variable winds are common and impossible to beat. You know how it goes: You check the wind and it blows out of the south. Then you climb into your stand and notice the wind hits you from the north. That is an unbeatable circumstance. As the old saying goes, "You don't have a prayer."

Approaching fronts may cause variable winds, but they can also cause sudden changes in the barometer, prompting deer to move without warning. With this in mind, the hunter should still consider being out there even if it appears that a variable wind could cost him. I certainly don't give up a hunting opportunity when an inconsistent wind develops, but I do choose my ambush locations a little more discreetly.

Forget about ambush sites located smack-dab in the middle of hills, hollows, and the big timber when variable winds are possible. Instead, select a site that is located in an open area. Fencelines along agricultural areas are ideal locations, provided cover and the right deer trail exist.

You should also consider hunting the fringes of big timber, or funnels and narrow grown-up travel corridors when competing against variable winds. The wind direction will be much more reliable than in dense areas surrounded by timber.

AVOID OVER-CLEARING

I'm a fanatic when it comes to clearing too much. I love many of the fabulous products that allow us to clear shooting lanes and extra debris around our stands, but those nifty little pruners and saws can get you in a whole lot of trouble if you are not careful.

The question is, how easily will a deer notice changes to an area? I've spent enough time around captive deer to understand that a whitetail knows every little detail of its home area perfectly. I've seen bottle-fed captive deer that have no fear of people stomp and then go berserk over a little white bucket that happened to be set down in a place it never was before. Deer are not fond of changes and there's always an adjustment period when a change occurs. The problem is, in the time it takes a buck to get used to the changes in your hunting area, he is likely to be long gone and out searching for does.

Over-clearing is not as big a

The most effective shooting lane is one that allows the surrounding cover to remain as natural-looking to deer as possible. *Photo by Fiduccia Enterprises.*

problem for firearm hunters as it is bowhunters, but it is still a problem. Even though a gun hunter might not be concerned about shooting lanes, he could decide to clear an area for better visibility, and any clearing near your ambush site can be disastrous.

When clearing shooting lanes for the archery season, I prefer opening only a few. A 360-degrees circle of openness is not necessary. Cover hides you from the deer's line of vision even if you are in a tree stand. Cover also allows you to draw your bowstring without getting spotted.

Whitetails quickly notice a major change in an area and could even avoid it for a long time. For this reason, clear only what is necessary around your ambush site.

When clearing, get help if possible. You can remain in the stand while someone on the ground clears the limbs you point out. One person on the ground always has a tendency to clear too much, so it's always better if you have a bird's-eye view.

Once you finish clearing, move the debris away from your ambush site so it goes unnoticed. If you happen to have a brushpile close by, you can leave it there without arousing suspicion. However, I would not suggest you start a new brush pile close to your ambush site.

There are many other things you can do to remain undetected, but I've covered the most important ones. A mature whitetail buck is not necessarily a forgiving animal when survival is at stake. That's no big deal if you don't want a second chance after making a mistake. Just remember that you are not a natural part of a big buck's environment, no more than he would be walking around in downtown Chicago. For this reason, you must do everything you can to always keep him guessing as to where you've been, where you are, and where you will be. ■

Primary Rut

9

Decoding the Rut

Throughout this book, I have mentioned several times that anyone—at just about any location—can kill a buck during the primary rut. Bucks are on the move, making sure that any hunter, regardless of how much they know about hunting deer, can enjoy success.

Some hunters only get in the woods during the primary rut, knowing this is the best opportunity to take a trophy whitetail. That's understandable, but hunting only during the peak-breeding season will not make you a knowledgeable deer hunter. It might make you a better woodsman and all-around outdoorsman, but there's too much left unsaid about deer during the primary rut.

With this emphasized for the 500th time in this book, I should mention that I still love hunting the primary rut. I look forward to it during the pre-rut, and I dread the arrival of the post-rut season. Consider how hard you might work during the pre-rut period, yet never get close to shooting a trophy buck. We're all entitled to compensation for our hard work. The primary rut is the time to be compensated.

In 1996, my son John hunted hard during the archery pre-rut season, hoping to get a crack at a wall-hanger. It didn't happen. However, when the firearm season debuted, which was timed with the peak of the rut, he tagged a buck that grossed just over 164 Boone and Crockett inches.

I should point out that you could be the luckiest during the primary rut if you have an understanding of how the rut unfolds. And knowing the habits of breeding whitetails could make you lucky sooner than otherwise.

This section discusses the breeding cycle that occurs during

Photoperiodism refers to the length of time sunlight is available. A buck's testosterone level rises as the amount of light decreases.

Once the breeding begins, bucks start taking chances, moving into open areas at any hour of the day in search of estrous does.

the primary period, which lasts about ten to fourteen days. That's when most of the does are bred. However, every area has one "peak-rut day" governed by latitude, when breeding peaks. It could be mid-November in your area or perhaps December 30, but it typically falls within the same time frame each year, and experienced hunters can narrow it down to within three to five days.

In the northern U.S., most of the whitetail breeding occurs between November 5 and 20. It is about thirty to sixty days later in the southern part of the country.

Photoperiodism plays a key role in determining the breeding period. Photoperiodism is the term used to define shorter days, or the decrease of sunlight. It's a gradual and slow process that begins after the longest day of the year in summer. The effects of photoperiodism are two-fold. First, the buck's testosterone level rises throughout the process. As pointed out earlier in the book, bucks will breed whenever opportunity allows ; they just need to be in the right place at the right time. But if only the time is right, they will go looking for the right place.

Some hunters wonder if an onset of cloudy days would affect the arrival date of the breeding cycle. I know of no research to support that. In fact, in the forty years I have hunted whitetails and observed their breeding cycle in the Midwest, I can say that the peak has never fluctuated by more than seventy-two hours. Granted, weather might affect deer movement and buck activity, but I don't believe it has any affect on the breeding cycle.

Determining the peak day is not that hard to do. Typically, when the rut peaks the bucks run rampant. You will see them at all hours of the day, often crossing fields and skirting the edges in search of a doe about to breed. All you need to do is be out there in the woods, and in some cases you can determine the peak by way of vehicle.

You should understand that a high testosterone level, most common in dominant, mature bucks, allows them to establish hierarchy prior to the rut. Mature bucks do most of the breeding. When photographing whitetails, I have observed many a doe running away from subordinate bucks, only to allow a dominate buck to breed her a short time later.

Researchers have noted that when mature bucks are in short supply, a doe might leave her home range to find Mr. Right. Keep in mind that many areas are short of trophy whitetails. Thus, traveling does might prevent a big buck from coming into your hunting area. Naturally, the more mature bucks you have around your hunting area, the better the chance a trophy will show up . . . and the does in your area will attract mature bucks.

Does are also affected by photoperiodism. When it peaks, they go into estrous—often termed "in-heat"—due to a dramatic increase in estrogen production. This reaction is timed with ovulation, making certain eggs will be present and fertilized by the buck's sperm. Research has shown that estrous does are, in a sense,

Just as photoperiodism affects bucks, it affects does, causing a rise in estrogen, and eventually the estrous period during which they breed.

like rutting bucks. They become restless and move much more often than they did during the pre-rut period.

There are other factors worth noting about estrous does. They urinate more often and, more importantly, their urine contains a scent that tells bucks they are ready to breed. A doe will stay in estrous for about twenty-four hours. If she is not impregnated when the estrous cycle ends, she will not allow a buck to breed her again until the next cycle in about twenty-seven to twenty-nine days. I read where one Alabama doe had her second estrous cycle twenty-one days after the first, while a doe in Minnesota had her second thirty days after the first.

It's true that poorly nourished bucks and does might not have typical breeding cycles. Most unhealthy bucks will reach a testosterone peak several days or weeks before the peak-rut day. A doe could come into estrous several days or weeks earlier as well.

Previously, I mentioned that the primary rut cycle is a short period of about two weeks or less, but that is not carved in stone. One Michigan study of healthy penned deer showed the breeding cycle of 174 does lasted from November 2 to December 21. Worth noting, though, is that more than eighty percent of the does mated during the last three weeks in November.

The breeding cycle always ends abruptly, particularly when it comes to mature does—those one-and-a-half years or older. Fawns, or six-month-old does, sometimes breed their first winter, but usually not as early as mature does. (The rutting habits of late-breeding does are discussed in Section III.)

In his book *Quality Deer Management,* renowned outdoor writer and whitetail consultant Charles Alsheimer divides the rut into three phases: seeking, chasing, and breeding. He claims that similarities exist in each phase, yet different habits are also common. How right he is!

For instance, bucks might cover a tremendous amount of ground just before the breeding begins. Yet once a buck discovers an estrous doe, he might stay in a given area for more than a couple of days.

When a doe comes into estrous, a mature buck will find her. In fact, he usually finds her a day or two before the breeding begins. I once observed a huge eleven-point buck with the same doe three days in a row. I never saw him breed her, but I made it a point to return to the same ambush location daily, assuming the hot doe would get hotter. She did, and I shot the buck on the third day.

Other bucks will be around as well, even if they are not fully mature. Several times when hunting, I have observed as many as five bucks after the same doe. In some non-hunting areas while photographing whitetails, I've seen even more. On one November morning when I left my stand and walked to a field, I saw five bucks hanging around a single doe. One carried a large eight-point rack while the others were still waiting to see their second birthday. I knelt in the bushes for nearly an

A dominant buck will threaten a subordinate by displaying aggressive behavior. He lowers his ears and his hair stands up as he slowly approaches. It's usually enough of a show to send a smaller buck away.

hour while the bucks chased the doe from one end of the field to the other.

Does are often injured and sometimes killed by the antlers of a mature buck that becomes aggravated while waiting to breed. It is not common, but he might jab her in the backend, causing injury.

As mentioned previously, subordinate bucks seldom breed. However, it does happen, particularly when several does come into estrous simultaneously. In some cases, a mature buck might be particular about his partner (which occurs more often than you think). If no mature buck arrives, an estrous doe might breed with a younger buck. In other words, being a mature buck does not necessarily come with exclusive breeding rights. It only gives him first choice.

A mature buck will keep the other bucks at bay, so to speak, staying close to the breeding doe and leaving her only to chase off a subordinate buck when necessary. Even then, he seldom runs very far. If he forces the smaller buck fifty to one hundred yards away, he's often content. It's also true that sometimes a mature buck won't have to run a small buck away. They often just lower their ears and walk toward the youngster with a ready-to-kill look in their eyes. When showing this aggression, their hair stands up on their backs—an unmistakable message that causes most small bucks to turn and walk away.

Bucks lip curl after sniffing doe urine. A doe does not have to be in estrous to cause a buck to lip curl, however.

Subordinate bucks are usually the ring leaders when most of the doe chasing occurs. This behavior goes on throughout the pre-rut period, but it is strongest just before a doe comes into estrous. Mature bucks seldom chase does until the primary rut period.

Just before the actual breeding of most does begins, mature bucks move consistently in dense areas where does commonly bed during daylight hours, sniffing beds to see if a doe is "Ready Freddy."

Hunters sometimes claim to have seen a buck trailing a doe, but going the wrong way. I doubt that backtrailing occurs in error, because a whitetail's nose is too good not to know a hot trail and the direction a doe is traveling. I do believe, though, that he will sometimes backtrail a doe in hopes of finding her bed to see if she is about to come into estrous.

Just before copulation occurs, a buck will approach the south end of a doe to scent her and determine how close he is to breeding her. He will often try to stimulate her by licking her vulva.

When a buck mounts a doe, he lowers his chin and slides it along her back. His forelegs rest just behind her shoulders. This does not pin her down, however. Occasionally, she will pull away when he first attempts to breed her.

I have observed whitetails breeding on several occasions. Copulation takes only about ten to twenty seconds, but is often repeated within a few minutes. I saw one buck breed a doe, and then breed her two more times in a ten-minute period. He would have bred her again, except the doe would not allow it—possibly because she felt pain and discomfort. About one hour later, however, he did breed her once more.

Lip curling is a trademark of the primary rut, but not limited to that period. Lip curling is an expression displayed by a buck after scenting a doe's urine. He extends his head upward, opens his mouth and rolls his lower lip forward. However, a doe does not have to be in estrous, or even near estrous. I have seen bucks lip curl after smelling doe urine during the off-season.

Hunters often become excited when they see a doe with a tail in the horizontal position, convinced she is in estrous. While it is true that many hunters have shot trophy bucks following a doe with a stiffened tail, I'm not so sure it is always a sign that the doe is willing to breed. Many times, I have seen does with their tails pointing outward, either briefly, when defecating, or just because they favor this position for no obvious reason. It could also be that the doe has already bred.

Research has shown that a doe's vulva has contractions after she has bred, which causes her tail to rise and sometimes stay that way off and on for a long time, up to a couple of days. Thus, when you see a doe with a tail in the horizontal position, you could be, as the old saying goes, "A day late …."

Vocalization is strongest during the primary rut. A buck will commonly send the grunt-snort-wheeze signal to other bucks, especially when breeding is close.

During the primary rut, a mature buck will seldom feed, although water remains important to him. I saw one mature buck walk away from a breeding doe to drink from a ditch about two hundred yards away. The two deer had been in a grown-up field for several hours. They had bred on a few occasions, and both had bedded a couple of times. When the buck left the doe, she was feeding, but he never browsed on the lush vegetation once. When he left to go to water, he was only gone about ten minutes, and she was out of his sight for only about five minutes as he passed through thick vegetation and walked down a steep bank. After drinking, the buck casually walked back to the doe.

As the rut winds down, mature bucks will move less and less. Subordinate bucks, though, continue to move consistently for several days in areas where hunting pressure is low, seeming to know that the dominant bucks are resting up. They also seem to know that they could stumble onto that late-breeding doe (not likely, however).

Bucks lose a tremendous amount of body weight during the rut—some as much as twenty-five percent or more. When the breeding ends, they go on a feeding binge that opens the door to post-rut hunting tactics. But during those glorious primary rutting days, a little knowledge can lead to a lot of luck.

It has been suggested that bucks typically weigh more and have bigger antlers if they don't breed much. I would think that in areas where there are fewer does, bucks might also lose less weight and sport smaller headgear because the rut is

This buck is following the trail of a doe. Hunters sometimes spot bucks backtrailing a doe, but this often occurs because a rutting buck will check the beds to locate an estrous doe.

extremely strenuous. They have to move more to find estrous does, and the competition is sure to be a problem because nearly every buck will end up pursuing the same doe.

Your chances of tagging a trophy buck during primary rut might be better if you don't have several does to every buck, which is precisely why does should be harvested. It boils down to quantity vs. quality. Lots of does (particularly a healthy herd) will produce many fawns. This means you will have more deer in your area, but it doesn't necessarily mean that your chance of intercepting a mature buck is that good. Studies have shown that the fewer does there are, the more bucks move. Hunters have shown that the more the bucks move, the better their chances of tagging a trophy.

Speaking of harvesting does, the best time to do so is not during the peak rut or during the primary rut unless you have tagged your buck. Shooting a doe could promptly spoil an area for a few days. Besides, who's to say the right buck isn't trailing the doe you shoot? You just can't beat the post-rut period for harvesting does.

As for big bucks trailing does, I've always suspected that other hunters have enjoyed more of this good fortune than I have. I consistently hear stories about guys who watched a doe pass, then had a whopper buck come walking through minutes or sometimes hours later. I don't mind telling you, I'm still waiting for that to happen to me. The chances of the right buck trailing a doe rest a little upon Lady Luck. If you are seeing your share of does, you know you are sitting in the right ambush location. But if you are not seeing the does, you can't blame Lady Luck alone.

Now that you have an understanding of the primary rut, you know that the rutting habits of bucks and does are totally different than their behaviors at any other time of the year. You should also know that there's much more between the lines, such as scraping and other rutting factors. These habits are your ticket to tagging a mature buck during the primary rutting season.

This buck is nervous about something. Note his tightly tucked tail. Even a doe in estrous won't keep a mature buck from seeking cover when he smells danger.

10
Opening Day vs. Last Day

I t's no big secret. The first day of the firearm season in many states and provinces often debuts during the primary rut, and sometimes opening days occur at the peak of the breeding season. It's also true that many archery seasons carry into the primary rut. This is good news for all hunters, and it provides game and fish departments the best opportunity to manage deer herds.

However, for just a moment stop and think ahead to the end of the hunting season. In many areas, the last opportunity of the year also occurs during the primary rut. In a way, that's good news, too, since it gives you one last hope if you were unsuccessful earlier. In reality though, the last day never compares with the first. Most hunters fully realize that after opening day of the firearm season, their

Indiana deer hunter Mark Williams took this 154-inch buck on opening morning of the firearm season at the peak of the breeding season.

chances of tagging a wall hanger are slim—even if the primary rut is still operating at full speed.

The firearm season lasts for several weeks in some areas. In others, it's a matter of days. Nevertheless, if hunting pressure exists, it really doesn't matter how long the firearm season lasts. Opening day and last day call for different tactics. Even if you are bowhunting, you often need to apply tactics similar to those that the firearm hunter relies on.

In Indiana, I'm used to a sixteen-day firearm season. That's not as long as the season lasts in some areas, but it's better than in neighboring Illinois, where I also hunt. The Prairie State hosts a three-day gun season during the primary rut and a four-day season later when the rut is on the downhill slide. Because of the short gun seasons, more bucks will survive in Illinois than in those states and provinces where firearm seasons are longer. However, one thing about opening day is the same in all areas: It's absolutely the best time of the year to shoot a monster buck.

On opening day of the firearm season, you have the opportunity to "get 'em while they're hot." Consider that the does are breeding, or about to. The bucks, meanwhile, are doing what comes natural, covering ground furiously in search of does, often moving at all hours of the day.

Many deer hunters select opening-day ambush locations in areas they suspect bucks might run to, or those where a buck is likely to travel after being spooked. In other words, they don't worry about patterning deer. Instead, they prefer to pattern other hunters, relying on them to push deer into certain locations, or along those travel routes deer will use when pressured.

I might as well tell you right up front that I don't hunt big bucks using the previously mentioned tactics. They are not especially productive methods as far as I'm concerned. Certainly, the more hunting pressure in the area, the better your chance a buck might head for particular parts of the country. It's also true that the more hunting pressure in the area, the better the chances of a buck getting pushed past your ambush site. However, when hoping to cash in on a mature buck, it's much more productive, and more enjoyable, in my opinion, to hunt the area that will most likely attract him. Like many hunters, I agree that it's better to allow the deer to function normally. Hunting pressure will arrive soon enough without additional help.

Consider a huge ten-pointer I shot several years ago on opening day. For my ambush location, I had selected a stand of oaks where the acorns were dropping consistently. Normally, the acorns had dropped and most were already consumed by the time the firearm season began. But unusual weather patterns had contributed to a late nut mast, and the familiar pocket of red oaks first started shedding acorns just a few days before the firearm season began. I was lucky enough to find them, and even luckier to capitalize on their mast.

Before the pressure begins, bucks will be on the lookout for estrous does.

When I discovered the oaks, I found numerous droppings over a large area near them, as well as several tracks and riddled trails close by. I knew the does were visiting the oaks consistently and that there might not be a better set up on opening day of the firearm season. It looked like the perfect place for an anxious buck to find a hot doe.

Thirty minutes after dawn, a doe and fawn came to the oaks. They fed for about fifteen minutes, never once looking behind them to indicate they were being followed by you know who. Eventually, they left for their bedding area. No bucks pursued them, and I could only remain hopeful that one would before my opening-morning hunt closed for another year.

That was the end of the action for the next three hours, until two button bucks walked in to dine on the numerous acorns. I watched them for at least thirty minutes before becoming bored and starting to hope they would soon leave. Thank goodness they kept me in the tree, though.

Noticing one of the fawns look toward a hill one hundred yards to the south , I suddenly saw a buck coming toward them, and me. As he traveled the valley along the side of the hill, I thought he was small. My opinion quickly changed when he topped the hill and I saw his huge headgear. I knew my patience near the oaks would soon pay off. The two young deer stayed put until the ten-pointer was within forty yards, then they turned and rapidly walked away. A moment later, my gun roared and the buck dropped. I shot the 145-inch deer only ten yards from my stand.

This opening-day buck did exactly what I had hoped he would. He came in to the hot oaks—not to feed, however. After a long night of searching for does, it was a stopover for him as he headed for his bedding area. Perhaps he had been there sometime during the night, before I arrived on stand, hoping to find a breeding doe. Perhaps he would have shown up again late that afternoon. Perhaps he had been there on numerous other occasions. Who knows?

What I do know is that this opening-day hunting technique provides one of the best opportunities to shoot a trophy buck.

Naturally, that's easier said than done, which is why I

The author took this buck near a stand of oaks the first morning of the firearm season. The 145-inch buck came to the food source late in the morning, knowing good and well it was one of the best places to find a hot doe. *Photo by Vikki L. Trout.*

suggest that, before opening day, you look for areas where the does will be—a food source or, perhaps, a hot trail. The idea is to hunt where the bucks will likely be, and that is wherever the does are. Of course, we're still only talking about opening day and the primary rut. This tactic does not apply to pressured bucks.

When scouting for opening day, you'll probably find your share of buck sign—rubs and scrapes. In a later chapter, I discuss hot scrapes and those that sometimes pay off during the primary rut in more detail, but as for rubs, forget them. They usually only raise false hope.

I talked about rubs and rub lines in Section I and how they can help you tag a mature buck in the pre-rut period. They could provide a link to a certain trail or bedding area, allowing you to pattern the buck. I also stressed that rubs can tell you where a buck will soon be. However, during the primary rut they can be quite misleading. First, consider that the rubs you find could have been made months, weeks or only several days earlier. Second, even if you find rubs made just before or during the primary rut, you have no way of knowing whether the responsible buck is still in the neighborhood. He might have been there twenty minutes before, but he can cover a lot of ground in that short time. Always assume that a rub found during the primary rut was made by a buck that could be two hundred yards off, a mile away, or more. It's true that many bucks continue to rub trees throughout the primary rut. However, rubs made during the breeding season are not at all as dependable as those in the pre-rut.

It boils down to this: You can pattern bucks during the primary rut only if you pattern the does first. Watch for tell-tale sign to find out where the does are spending their time. Look for fresh droppings in feeding areas and along trails. The bucks will visit the same food sources and follow the same trails.

Once you find the does, plan to spend your opening-day ambush location in the same area. That's the best strategy when the primary rut is underway. When and if that fails, you must go to Plan B.

Plan B begins after opening day. Again, let me stress that if the hunting pressure is light, you could get by using opening-day tactics on the second and third day. However, many hunters already know that their chances of tagging a big buck drop drastically after the first day of the firearm season.

The major percentage of the firearm harvest occurs on opening day. That's also when most mature bucks are shot. These statistics are

Rubs always look appealing when scouting, and while they can pay off during the pre-rut period and allow you to pattern a buck, seldom do they provide results for opening day of the firearm season when the breeding has begun, or is about to. *Photo by Vikki L. Trout.*

Find the does first and then plan your ambush location nearby. However, this tactic might be good for a short time only, and in some cases, only on opening day.

It doesn't take long for the deer to find out that something is up. Sometimes, only hours into the firearm season, many bucks go into hiding, moving less in daylight hours with each passing day.

understandable, since it is also when the most hunters head for the woods. Nevertheless, it's also true that most big bucks won't be educated until opening day ends, by which time, they have heard the shooting and, in some cases, encountered hunters. I don't think any mature buck actually realizes that opening day of the firearm season has begun. I do believe, though, that some inner "click" causes them to immediately sharpen their survival instincts. Folks who are out there every opening day, like you and me, have made this complimentary life-saving contribution.

The key is to know when to change your hunting strategies. Although the primary rut is still underway, mature bucks will eventually forego traveling at any hour of the day. Moreover, they will not pass through open areas where they once took risky chances in hopes of finding a doe. Consider, too, that in most cases the hunting pressure will also change the habits of the does. Like bucks, the does have instincts that let them know their environment has suddenly changed. Once this happens, it won't do you much good to hunt the areas where the does once were. They will avoid the usual trails and hot foods like the plague. That's when the bucks start hiding and looking for does only in deserted areas.

After the hunting pressure changes the habits of both bucks and does, you should consider moving into the densest cover. The thickest cover is where a whitetail wants to be any time security becomes an issue. That goes for does, subordinate and mature bucks.

I will often set up a stand in or near the densest cover before the firearm season begins, or just after—a tactic I pre-schedule, just in case it's needed. Once the pressure intensifies, the mature bucks will enforce stricter moving restrictions. They will bed down earlier in the morning and not leave their bedding areas as early in the afternoons. Plan B depends on your ability to find the most attractive bedding areas and set up ambush locations nearby.

Later in this section, you will read more about those areas that appeal to pressured bucks in the primary rut. But for now, it's important that you understand the differences between the first and last days of the firearm season. All too often hunters waste their time in the late gun season because they used the same tactics they did on opening day. Also, too many hunters think they can pattern bucks for opening day when the primary rut has begun. Wrong! Your best opening-day strategy is patterning the does.

Although I have pointed out that you should change tactics *after* opening day, it doesn't necessarily mean you can't enjoy success using the same ambush tactics on another day. Yes, it's possible that bucks will get into the rutting frenzy and move consistently, just as they did when searching for does on opening day. All you need for this to happen is a little help from Mother Nature. ▪

11
Cold Fronts and Moon Phases

During the primary rut, mature bucks quickly become discouraged when hunting pressure intensifies. This has an effect on morning and evening buck activity in daylight hours, and causes changes in the habits of does. However, there are natural phenomena that occur each year, prompting whitetail bucks to get with the program. If the hunter recognizes the phases that trigger bucks to move, he can enjoy an opportunity comparable to opening day at the peak of the breeding season.

Most hunters share one thing in common—a preference for hunting on days

Although most hunters prefer to be out when favorable weather conditions exist, research indicates that bucks may move more as a cold front approaches.

with radiant sunrises and sunsets. Along with these, we like crisp temperatures and no wind. But are these really the ultimate hunting conditions?

COLD FRONTS AND BAROMETER CRASHES

Ideal weather usually occurs when the barometer is steady. However, research indicates that deer may move more frequently when the barometer is unstable, especially if it drops drastically. Many hunters also report seeing more deer when such a weather front approaches.

I still remember a particular November hunt several years ago. It wasn't what you would have called a good day to be perched in a tree. There had been a warm southerly breeze just the day before, but now I had to fight uncontrollable shivers brought on by a strong north wind, rapidly plummeting temperature and a light drizzle. Perhaps that is why I didn't see the huge buck slithering past my stand until I caught a glimpse of movement in my peripheral vision. I shouldered the gun and attempted to find him in the crosshairs of my scope, but before I could locate him, the deer disappeared into a thicket.

That incident remains vivid in my mind for good reason. A few moments after the buck vanished from my sight, I heard a shot several hundred yards to the east.

In planning hunts, many of us don't think about the barometer. Research suggests, however, that changing barometric pressure can signal good hunting.

My dad had also braved the brutal weather, and was rewarded for this daring venture. His gun dropped the huge nine-pointer as it passed by him.

In recent years, I have come to look forward to the somber days whenever the rut is close or in progress. In fact, I can hardly resist heading for the woods on a nasty day. It had been no surprise to see that buck sneaking past, and no real shock when I heard dad fire minutes later. The conditions can be almost unbearable when a north wind blows in, but I have discovered that miserable weather can considerably improve my chance of tagging a buck, even if hunting pressure has sent him into hiding. This realization has made it easier for me to stay out there, regardless of what Mother Nature does.

For many years I have kept records of deer sightings, and I've tracked my harvests and the conditions that existed on a given day, including changes in barometric pressure. I've seen a strong increase in buck movement when a big change in barometric pressure occurs.

Dr. Grant R. Woods, a wildlife biologist who has studied deer movement for a number of years, has collected data indicating that deer move much more than usual when the barometric pressure changes by four or five points. Such a change commonly occurs when a cold front approaches. Grant said that hunters should look forward to the first cold front of the season, since deer are always prompted to move. However, he added that deer move and feed heavily only as long as the barometric pressure declines. He bases this fact on studies that show increased deer sightings when the barometer drops. However, a rising barometer usually does not hold as much promise for hunters.

"A rising barometer is trickier than a falling barometer," Woods said. "This can occur when you go from an extended low that has been around for several days to a high-pressure system moving in. Under these conditions, you just don't get a big change in deer movement. In fact, any change is usually a gradual one."

How Bucks Respond

So, how does all this affect bucks? First, consider the rutting activity of bucks and then the hunting pressure that might have set them back. Next, consider the approaching cold front and the falling barometer. The weather conditions trigger deer movement, causing them to feed heavily, and bucks know that the does will be up and moving, which stimulates them to move, too.

While photographing whitetails on numerous occasions, I've seen does in fields feeding heavily as a cold front approached. Watching them, I often spot bucks. Most of the time, the antlered deer cared less about eating than about checking out the does. When hunting, I've observed a similar effect when bad weather approached: does moving and browsing, and bucks moving in search of does. For this reason, I believe that the approaching cold front and falling barometer cause a rise in the buck's testosterone level.

An approaching cold front can trigger strong winds and a drop in barometric pressure, causing all deer to move. The does move to feed, and the bucks move because they know the does are out and about.

The deer hunter should understand exactly what prompts deer to feed heavily when a cold front approaches. Precipitation and wind are the two primary factors that apply. Deer want to feed before the hardest rain, heaviest snow or strongest wind arrives so they can stay bedded while the nastiest weather prevails. That's not to say that some precipitation and wind will not be present as the front approaches. On the contrary, in the episode I mentioned previously, the cold front had not yet arrived, but it was knocking at the door with the constant drizzle and gusty winds. My idea of prime time to be in the deer woods.

Make no mistake: An approaching warm front accompanied by its own wind and rain will also cause the barometer to fall. Do not count on an increase in buck movement when a Southerly approaches, however. The barometer tends to fall fast before a cold front, but bucks don't move as well when a warm front approaches because the barometric pressure doesn't change as rapidly. Logically, we can also assume that bucks are move comfortable when cooler temperatures exist.

According to a meteorologist I spoke with, the more change there is in temperature, the more rapidly the barometer falls. For instance, let's say the barometer has remained steady for a lengthy period and the temperature has been in the 60s and 70s. Along comes a fast-moving cold front that drops temperatures into the 20s and 30s. The barometer will fall several points rapidly, and the bucks will move.

If, however, it has been in the 40s and 50s, and the approaching cold front drops the temperatures to the 30s and 40s, the barometer will not fall as much or as rapidly. You can be sure bucks will not move as much as they would have if a stronger cold front was on the way.

TIMING IS CRUCIAL

If you get in the woods as the cold front settles on the area, more than likely you will miss the hottest action. The best hunting occurs when the cold air first bumps against the warm air, and the temperatures start to fall. It could happen at prime hunting time in the morning or afternoon, at night or during the mid-day hours. The point is, you should already be hunting when it hits (excluding the dark hours, of course).

The incident that I mentioned earlier involved perfect timing. The temperature was about seventy-five degrees (quite unusual) and the wind had begun to intensify. I remember talking to my dad earlier that day. We had not seen many bucks, and had blamed that on previous hunting pressure and warm weather. We both arrived on stand earlier than usual that somber afternoon, and I'm convinced that the front had given him a better chance of harvesting a buck than he would have had the next day, after the front settled on the area.

WHERE TO HUNT

It's hard to say exactly where you should hunt when a cold front approaches. Personally, I have had the best results hunting afternoons and sticking to food sources. When favorable weather exists, deer may not show up close to a food source in daylight hours. But that can change when the barometer is falling. Then deer may arrive at a food source much earlier than normal. The hunting pressure will probably be lighter than usual, which might help get the deer to you without disturbance.

Earlier in this book I men-

When the barometer starts falling, deer often start feeding earlier in the day than normal. *Photo by Fargason Technologies/Scentite Blinds.*

109

tioned the massive twelve-point Alberta buck I rattled into bow range. A light rain, coupled with wind gusts, did not dampen the spirits of the buck that responded to my rattling. That evening I also watched another buck chase does—something I had not seen previously in the five days I had been pursuing whitetails in this area. My ambush location was along the edge of a field where deer had come to feed.

Moon Effects and Rutting Activity

For many years, deer hunters have wondered how whitetails are affected by moon phases. We've all heard various opinions about the full moon and new moon, but with little research to back up these interesting discussions, we can only wonder what to expect when hunting.

We do know that one full lunar cycle takes about twenty-nine days. During this period, the moon goes through four phases, including the new moon, when the nights are darkest, and the full moon, when the nights are brightest. It is popularly believed that deer become nocturnal during a full moon, which has led many hunters to think that much of the breeding occurs at night.Thus, one could assume the best time to kill a buck is only during the new moon. While this theory makes sense, veteran hunters will tell you there is far more to the story.

Full Moon and New Moon

Many hunters claim that we should never assume that deer become nocturnal during the full moon. Like others, I strongly believe that they will lay up and move less during daylight hours, but timing of the new moon is the real issue.

Let's say the peak of the rut typically arrives November 10. If the full moon occurs in late October, there will be a new moon in early November. Thus, does might come into estrous a few days earlier and cause an increase in buck movement. The same principle applies if the full moon arrives just before the peak of the breeding season. The hottest action will occur a few days later.

Everything can backfire if the full moon falls about one month before the peak of the breeding season. When it does, hunters can count on another full moon during the heart of the primary rut, a scenario that could mean a hunter will see fewer bucks during the daylight hours.

David Hale of Knight & Hale Game Calls once told me that when hunters experience the full moon during the primary rut, they should rely on other tactics. It only makes

If the full moon arrives during the primary rut, try hunting during the midday hours.

sense, he says, that hunters consider the rut less visible. Buck movement is likely to become sporadic and inconsistent, as if the primary rut had arrived, but it hasn't.

Many seasoned hunters now say it is no longer the early morning and late evening hours that produce action if the moon is full during the primary rut. In fact, these hunters claim that midday action can be unbeatable—usually at its best action between 10 A.M. and 2 P.M.

I sincerely believe that we should never decide to hunt or not to hunt based on a particular moon phase. Weather patterns and hunting pressure are probably more significant when it comes to determining when bucks do and do not move (especially during the primary rut).

Many veteran hunters believe deer move and feed heavily at night during the full moon, laying up before the first light of day begins.

One individual I discussed this with explained that the guy who can hunt quality private land will see more buck activity during the full moon than the guy who is hunting crowded public lands during the new moon, when the nights are darkest.

Serious hunters should consider reading *"Hunting Whitetails by the Moon,"* by Charles J. Alsheimer. It is a fact-filled book that provides an easy understanding of moon phases and effects, as well as technical information for pursuing deer during all phases of the rut.

When it comes to hunting a full moon, you could fall back on the old saying, "Expect the worst and hope for the best." When it comes to hunting the new moon, think about another proverb: "The right time is now."

I don't plan to forfeit any hunting time in the future, regardless of what moon phase exists, or whether the sun shines and the wind blows. You see, I like spending all the time I can in the woods, regardless of which phase of the rut we're in or hunting pressure around me. I might even find myself sitting near a hot scrape or two when the time is right. ▪

12

Hot Scrapes vs. Dead Scrapes

V eteran hunters are aware that scrapes are not limited to the primary rut. On the contrary, they begin showing up during early autumn. It's also true that big bucks have been harvested over scrapes several weeks before the primary rut. Thus, you might be wondering why you read very little about scrapes in Section I. I can explain that in one paragraph.

Scrape hunting is more productive during the primary rut just before, during, and just after the breeding. That word "just" is the key; the best time to shoot a mature buck over the right scrape, or scrapes, is limited to a few days. During the pre-rut period, I've

Scrapes begin showing up in early autumn but seldom provide action until the primary rut. *Photo by Vikki L. Trout.*

found it much more reliable to pattern mature bucks in other ways we've already discussed, such as rub lines, food sources and certain trails. With that out of the way, let's get on with how you can determine which scrapes are most likely to attract a mature buck.

Before I go any further about natural scrapes, you should be aware that I won't be discussing mock scrapes here, but they are covered in chapter 14, which provides ways to lure primary rutting bucks into range. For now, though, it's best to assume that scrapes are one of the least reliable ways to hang a trophy whitetail on the wall. Yes, I said "least." But don't jump ahead just yet. You see, natural scrapes offer more opportunities than mock scrapes.

Let's face it, a fresh scrape gets every whitetail hunter's adrenaline flowing and, for just a moment, flips on the "dream switch." Almost involuntarily, we imagine intercepting the ghostly buck that left his mark behind.

Such was the case a few years ago when I discovered no fewer than a dozen scrapes stretched along two hundred yards of a well-used trail. Several huge rubs were also present, prompting me to hang a stand in preparation for gun season, only days away. The scrape line was truly a sight to behold, and it followed a ridge of white oaks that were dropping acorns and attracting does. Equally important, there was a pocket of dense pines and honeysuckle nearby that, I knew, could well be a bedding area for the mature buck that had made the scrapes. More about what happened in a moment.

Locating scrapes or scrape lines is seldom difficult. If a hunter scouts enough, he or she can usually find buck sign. But coming across a potentially "hot" scrape line is seldom purely the result of luck. In fact, you can bet your luckiest camo hat that hunting near most scrapes will not produce positive results. Several factors determine whether or not a buck will visit the spot again, including where the scrapes are and how cautiously you investigated the area.

A seasonal rise in the buck's testosterone level prompts him to begin scraping, and this usually occurs during the pre-rut. But just how seriously should a hunter take these scrapes?

Research has shown that during the late summer and early fall, bucks will show signs of aggression toward each other. They begin scraping, but the scrapes left at this time are seldom more than territory markers used to advertise a particular buck's presence. Hunters generally find them before the primary rut, and they are often along the fringes of agricultural fields, logging roads and similar openings.

Territory scrapes, also known as boundary scrapes, typically show up along the fringes and roadbeds. However, seldom do these produce action. The author believes that the best scrapes are those that form a scrape line.

Some knowledgeable deer hunter first called them "boundary" scrapes eons ago—the perfect name. These boundary or territory scrapes seldom form a true scrape line, nor do they become scent stations revisited by bucks on a regular basis.

Researchers have also determined that as deer densities increase in an area, so do the number of scrapes. I certainly can attest to that. When hunting areas that hold several bucks, I always seem to locate scrapes earlier than I do in areas where there are fewer deer.

As the does approach sexual readiness, usually a few days before the peak of breeding, scrape activity intensifies. Many consistently successful hunters now believe this period is also the time to locate and hunt the hottest scrape lines for dominant bucks.

Several years ago, Dr. Larry Marchinton and his colleagues at the University of Georgia studied several groups of deer, noting that in pens containing bucks of age three and one-half and younger, the three and one-half-year-olds did most of the scraping. Younger bucks often avoid scraping early in the pre-rut period, because such scrapes serve as territory markers. Scraping close to the peak of the rut is usually done to facilitate scent communication with the does, but young bucks apparently have little or no desire to get aggressive with their elders.

If this is true, we can assume that fresh scrape lines found a few days preceding the peak of rut were made by dominant bucks ready to get down to serious business. But can a hunter count on these scrape lines to provide action?

I don't mind telling you that I have wasted a lot of time sitting in stands near a scrape or scrape lines. Many other veteran deer hunters would admit they have done the same. The bigger bucks just don't show up as often as we'd like.

According to Myles Keller, it could be because we often spoil a perfect opportunity before the hunt even begins. He says that a lot of scrape lines are of no use, because it's too tough to hunt them properly. Hunters must consider their approach to a scrape line and how much scent they leave near by. Moreover, even if they do everything perfectly, they still have to factor in the hunting pressure in that area.

Keller also notes that a single slip is all it takes to spoil a scrape line. Remember, we're talking about mature bucks. Once a dominant buck is alerted to your presence (or someone else's), you can count on him becoming more nocturnal, returning to the scrape line only during the dark hours. The avid hunter who visits the area consistently, meanwhile, sees that the scrape line is being freshened by the buck with some regularity, but fails to see the animal in daylight. Keller readily admits, however, that you can never be too careful when hunting a mature buck near a scrape line. He still finds himself making mistakes and forfeiting a particular location, simply because the buck discovered his presence.

Which scrapes offer the most potential, little ones or big ones? I've often heard hunters talk about finding scrapes as big as the hoods on a truck. I've found a few

(Above) The author has had much more success hunting scrapes when there are overhanging limbs that have been chewed and/or dismantled by bucks. (Below) However, even does will chew on overhanging limbs, sometimes because they want to know "who" was there, and possibly when they are nearing estrous.

like that myself. But after spending countless hours hunting over them through the years, I can't say that big scrapes will positively attract more bucks than little scrapes.

Big scrapes are often referred to as primary scrapes, and for good reason. A scrape that is four feet in diameter will be visited and freshened up more consistently than a two-foot scrape. Nonetheless, primary scrapes are still not as reliable as scrape lines.

I've had some of my best luck hunting scrapes beneath overhanging limbs that have been recently chewed and/or dismantled by the antlers of a buck. As you may know, the overhanging limbs I speak of are often rubbed with a buck's pre-orbital gland, which is on his forehead. These limbs, which typically hang about four to six feet above the ground directly above the scrape, are frequently licked, chewed and, many times, beaten to death with antlers. And don't think for a moment that does won't scent, lick or chew on such overhanging limbs. They do so quite often as the breeding gets close to peaking.

Many trees are not acceptable to bucks making a scrape and selecting an overhanging limb. Bucks usually prefer small deciduous trees, such as maples, pin oaks, dogwoods, fruit trees, ash and many others. Conifers are not favorites, but they are sometimes chosen.

I suspect the overhanging limb(s) are more important than the pawed area on the ground, having watched several deer pay little attention to the scrape itself but stop to smell the limb above. It happens throughout the primary rut and sometimes in the post-rut, several weeks after the scrape had been pawed. The overhanging

The author took this nine-pointer along a hot scrape line on the first day of the gun season. He found the scrapes during the primary rut, just days before the firearm season and the breeding debuted. *Photo by Vikki L. Trout.*

limbs serve as valuable scent posts to all deer, and their importance to the development of a hot scrape line is greater than the actual scrape on the ground.

One primary scrape with a chewed overhanging limb is likely tobe-come more of a dependable scent post than a big scrape that is only pawed. I would suggest you keep that in mind if you locate and want to hunt a primary scrape. Again, though, the line with several scrapes, where some have chewed and dismantled overhanging limbs, will be more likely to attract a big buck.

The scrape line mentioned near the beginning of this chapter included several scrapes with mutilated branches overhead, interspersed with other limbs that didn't show as much evidence of mature buck use. It pays to follow scrapes from one to the next to see how seriously bucks have taken the line as a whole.

After locating that line and setting up a portable stand, I avoided the area until opening day. About one hour after sunrise on the opener, I spotted a very respectable buck traveling along the scrape line. My slugster roared before he had a chance to check one of the scrapes less than forty yards from me. The nine-pointer ran only seventy-five yards before piling up within view of my stand.

When hunting scrapes, wear knee-high rubber boots with the pants tucked inside. Also, avoid getting too close to the scrape, and do not brush against foliage and limbs as you pass by. When a buck visits a scrape, his already keen sense of smell is turned on full power.

Because the area around a scrape line is unforgiving in terms of human scent, consider hunting the buck's travel route that connects to the scraping location. Myles Keller points out that dominant bucks are vulnerable when they travel to and from the scrapes, so if a hunter gravitates right to the scrape line, he can't afford to make the slightest mistake.

Therefore, Keller suggests piecing the scrape line together in relation to a buck's bedding site. He warns, however, that many variables can

Although it helps to wear rubber boots whenever you check a scrape, it's still very easy to leave scent behind and spoil a hunting opportunity. There's no need to get too close to a scrape. *Photo by Vikki L. Trout.*

Bucks will take more chances and cover much more ground in search of an estrous doe than they will to visit a hot scrape.

complicate hunting a travel route between a bedding area and a scrape line. For example, the number of does in the region can affect which trails the bucks use, and so can food sources. But you can often count on bucks to lay out a scrape line near or along the same routes does travel consistently.

Keller also noted that too much distance between the scrape line and the bedding area has a significant impact on a hunter's odds of success. An educated dominant buck simply will not travel very far during daylight hours to reach a red-hot scrape line.

But even if a mature buck is unlikely to take risks getting to a scrape line, he will travel far when he knows there's a pretty good chance of locating a breeding doe.

Scrape lines near funnels are often more productive, because when bigger bucks move during the daylight, they like to stay in the cover of an existing travel corridor. That is why one west-central Illinois outfitter prefers to hunt scrape lines that connect to funnels and bottlenecks between fields or fencelines.They are natural travel corridors that entice bucks to produce scrape lines. The bucks also know that a scrape line in these areas is more likely to be noticed by traveling does.

It is safe to say that no scrape line guarantees you a crack at a mature buck. I really believe that big whitetails will sacrifice breeding opportunities when they sense their survival is at stake. Even so, although it's safe to say that you could spend countless hours hunting dead scrapes, hunting a hot scrape line is one way to tag a trophy buck during the primary rut. That's providing you follow the previously mentioned guidelines and the standard set of rules I'll be discussing next. ■

Finding large tracks does not necessarily mean that a buck with large antlers left them. There is no better way to know a big buck exists than to see him. *Photo by Vikki L. Trout.*

Indiana bowhunter Dean Stallion took this eighteen-point, 189-inch buck during the pre-rut period. The buck came in near dusk, probably right after leaving its bedding area.

Grunting to a mature buck during the primary rut is one of the most reliable buck foolery methods hunters can employ.

Copulation lasts only a matter of seconds. However, a buck might breed a doe several times during a twenty-four-hour period.

A buck will scent, and sometimes lick, a doe's vulva just before breeding her.

The author took this huge Alberta deer just moments before dusk after rattling him in. The pre-rut buck had a Pope & Young gross score of 158 inches.

Rub lines commonly show up along fencelines, and in funnels and other travel corridors. It is also true that some rub lines occur in the same vicinity year after year.

Of the three ways to lure in a buck, decoying, grunting, and using scents, the author believes that grunting is the most effective–providing conditions are right. *Photo by Vikki L. Trout.*

When the hunting pressure intensifies, the bucks often head for no-man's land. However, these areas are sometimes close to or within the area where you already hunt.

Boot pads are often used to lay a scent trail. Their effectiveness is somewhat dependent on getting hotter, instead of colder, as you walk.

The author's son, John, took this monster buck at the peak of the breeding season. This is the time when many mature bucks make their last mistake.

Are fair-weather hunters missing out on the action? The author believes hunting success can skyrocket when the barometer takes a nose-dive. *Photo by Vikki L. Trout.*

Although this huge rub looks impressive, it was found during the primary rut when bucks were on the move. It did not provide any proof that a buck would make a return visit. However, had this rub connected to others, it could indicate a rub line and a frequently traveled route of a mature buck. *Photo by Vikki L. Trout.*

13
The Rut's Golden Rules

For just a moment, think about the number of times I've mentioned that it doesn't take a lot of skill to kill a trophy whitetail during the primary rut. All you need is a little luck. If there's a big one in the area, he could walk by you or some other hunter leaning against a tree two hundred yards away. However, things can still go terribly wrong for folks like you and I who work so hard to shoot a mature buck.

Most serious deer hunters spend countless hours reading about rut-hunting tactics that can be applied during the

Some hunters stick to one favorite ambush location where they were successful in the past. Keep an open mind, scout continuously and keep an eye on the does.

hunting season. Let's face it. In the past decade, there has been no shortage of articles on the subject. Some tell you how to hunt big bucks during all portions of the archery season, and there are stories that suggest proven drills—from luring bucks into range with a call, to hunting food sources, rub lines, scrapes and trails. You've already read about these topics in this book, and you'll read more about them in the chapters ahead. However, there's much more to the story.

Don't get me wrong. Articles that focus on tactics to fool rutting trophy bucks deserve the full attention of any serious trophy whitetail hunter. I read them with interest and I always keep an open mind. However, in most of these stories, at least six ingredients are commonly overlooked. In fact, regardless of the tactics you use, you must consider the following advanced common-sense topics if you hope to tag a trophy.

If you pattern the does during the primary rut, you will soon know if a big buck is in the area. However, be realistic and aware that quality private lands and remote public areas are the places big bucks prefer to roam in search of does.

1. PATTERN THE DOES

Despite our desire to hunt the same stomping grounds year after year, we must be sure that a trophy buck exists before deciding on a location. For instance, I have "favorite" areas that I know as well as the inside of my hunting closet (my wife disagrees). It's fun to hunt these areas because of past experiences and successes, but they are not necessarily the places to be during the rut. Simply said, a mature whitetail buck must roam this territory if I am to have a chance at intercepting him.

Getting stuck on an old spot can be detrimental to tagging a big buck. It's true that some favorite spots are almost always good places to be, and there are often good reasons why certain ambush locations consistently produce big bucks. Nonetheless, I would suggest keep one eye and ear open. Returning to a spot where you once took a trophy buck does not mean that lightning will strike twice in the same place.

Since "seeing is believing," many veteran bowhunters spend several hours watching food sources before the season. Take my good friend Tim Hillsmeyer, who has tagged several Pope and Young caliber bucks. Near dusk, Hillsmeyer often drives the roads in agricultural areas to locate big bucks, because the deer are visiting food sources in daylight hours. He also sets up near food sources with his binoculars handy, making certain that his presence is not detected while watching a particular field.

We discussed this tactic in the pre-rut section, but I mention it again to remind you that it's the existence of does that will attract bucks during primary rut. For this reason, you must know where the does will be. My point is, never limit your scouting to the pre-rut only. It's necessary to know exactly where a big buck is feeding and bedding if you want to pattern and kill him during pre-rut, and the same is true during the primary rut. It's necessary to know exactly where the does are feeding and bedding if you want to pattern and kill that same big buck you didn't shoot during the pre-rut.

2. BUILD LANDOWNER RELATIONS

It pays to have a good relationship with a landowner to tag a mature buck. It's no big secret; most successful trophy hunters pursue bucks on private lands that have little pressure. However, always consider gaining access to remote public ground that borders private land. Topographic maps are essential tools because many public-land bucks that survive year after year take refuge on or near adjoining private lands or hard-to-reach public ground when they feel pressured.

One item that will be helpful is an *Atlas and Gazetteer* by DeLorme, which provide topo maps of entire states in book format and are available at many sporting goods stores and bookstores. Finally, consider visiting the assessor's office in the county you hunt and purchasing a plat book to learn names of landowners.

3. AVOID TEMPTATION

If you really want to tag a trophy buck, common sense dictates that you must overlook bucks that have not yet reached their full potential. If you want to take only a buck that makes it into the record books, you must be able to judge antlers quickly and effectively in the field—on short notice. Of course, your idea of a trophy may differ from that of another hunter.

If the area you hunt offers numerous tags, it can be more difficult to pass a smaller buck that offers a shot. You could simply take

If you have more than one tag, you might hold off on shooting a lesser buck until you kill a trophy. Shooting just any buck can quickly spoil a hunting area for days to come.

the lesser buck and continue hunting for a wall-hanger. Unfortunately, though, bad news accompanies that practice.

First, consider that shooting any deer may disqualify the area as a potential trophy-producing site. When you shoot a deer in a particular region, you are sure to create a disturbance and leave behind scent—a situation that can become critical if you must track the deer for a long distance.

It is also possible that shooting the smaller buck will cause the does, which would have brought in the wall-hanger, to vacate the area. For this reason alone, many dedicated trophy hunters refuse to harvest a smaller buck just because they carry an "extra" tag. I don't have a problem with shooting does and small bucks when tags are available. I'm just saying that serious trophy hunters know where their priorities lie, and will wait until the time is right before shooting just any deer.

4. ERROR! ERROR!

Hillsmeyer claims that the most serious error a trophy hunter can make is scouting too often in the wrong places. He added that once a mature buck knows he is being hunted, the hunt might be over.

"Flush a buck out of hiding a time or two, and you can bet he's going somewhere else," said Hillsmeyer. "It's imperative that you do your scouting wisely, and then get in and out of an area without the buck knowing you are there."

I discussed this error in the pre-rut section, but I want to emphasize that a big buck will not appreciate getting bumped, even during the primary rut. If there are lots of does in the area, he might have spent several days there, even if it's unfamiliar territory. If you spook him, he'll probably take his chances looking for does elsewhere. Unlike subordinate bucks, mature bucks seldom "forgive and forget."

Since second shots at big bucks are rare, most trophy hunters never take chances when it comes to wind direction. In fact, hunting where the wind blows toward the area you expect the deer to come from is one way to insure you never see the buck you are waiting for. Thus, if the wind is wrong for your best ambush location, choose another even if it doesn't look as promising. It's better to sit in a bad location and not see any deer than to sit in a good location and spook one.

You should also pay close attention to air currents as you approach an ambush location, since they may differ from the actual wind direction. This can be accomplished easily by using scentless wind testing powder.

5. HIT IT HARD

I'm proud of several bucks I've taken that now hang on my living room wall, and I can honestly say that most of them did not come easy. It seems I always have to walk so many miles, hang so many stands, lose so much sleep and see so many other deer before my shooting opportunity comes. It's like having a quota that must

Tim Hillsmeyer points out that you must hunt hard, even during the primary rut, if you hope to get a chance at a trophy whitetail. He claims that even if you don't get him today, you'll learn something that will help you tomorrow.

be filled, except there still are no guarantees that I will enjoy success even when the quota is met. Many readers have probably had the same experiences.

The one thing I must always do is hunt hard. I make it a point to be out there every chance I get. In other words, "Never put off till tomorrow what you can do today." Sure, you could get lucky and have a wall-hanger walk past you any time, but when the primary rut is in high gear, "Tomorrow may never come." The odds are more in your favor for getting one "tomorrow" if you're out there today.

Hillsmeyer hit the nail on the head. "You can think of a thousand excuses why you shouldn't hunt, but the buck you are after is the one good reason to be there."

The best point Hillsmeyer makes about hunting often, though, is that you learn something each time you are there. You might not see the right buck today, but the experience could teach you something that will help you next time.

Logically speaking, we can safely assume that the whitetail's habits change considerably from week to week. They might not, but if they do and you are not aware of it, you'll be a day late when you head for the woods. Food sources change, as does hunting pressure. Each plays an important part in the whitetail's habits, and the hunter who is there at every opportunity may stay one step ahead of the bucks. Actually, change that to "does," the most important word in the rut dictionary when you are trying to kill a big buck.

Don't think for a moment that hunting from the perch is the only way to kill a trophy buck. The primary rut is one of the best times to choose a ground ambush location and to still-hunt.

6. CHOOSE VERSATILE AMBUSH LOCATIONS

It does help to stay on the move when it comes to ambush locations. I mentioned this in part I, but it's also valuable during the primary rut. Never limit yourself to hunting only from a tree stand when the breeding is underway.

Bowhunters are the world's worst about getting into a tree-stand rut, and some archers refuse to hunt from a ground site even when they switch to hunting with a firearm. Most assume they have no chance of killing a mature buck from the ground. I used to feel that way many years ago, but that was before I had taken several whitetails from a ground ambush.

Don't get me wrong. I'd rather be in a tree. I feel my best chance of intercepting a trophy buck is when I'm elevated in any portion of the hunting season. But when bucks are going crazy during the rut, why limit yourself to hunting from a tree? The rut is prime time to take a big buck from the ground, which means you can set up quickly in remote locations that have not been touched by others.

Then there's the still-hunting side of killing trophy bucks. Hillsmeyer, who usually hunts from a tree stand, has taken several bucks on the ground. He prefers a stiff wind and a quiet floor for still-hunting during the primary rut, when the foliage is thin, but he hunts on the ground during all phases of the rut. Ground hunting tactics and some of Hillsmeyer's tips are discussed in chapter 15.

You could say that hunting for a trophy buck is like baking a cake. You need to use the right methods and ingredients if you hope to get a topnotch finished product. In the case of hunting trophy whitetails during the primary rut, the scrapes, rubs, trails, and food sources of the does are the methods. The six previously mentioned topics are the ingredients. On the other hand, you might just try tempting a buck. ▪

14
Buck Foolery

Y
ou already know that the rut is the best time to take advantage of a mature buck. His survival instincts hit rock bottom, and a rutting buck's vulnerability is the key to luring him into bow or gun range. Easier said than done, but an effective tactic that many hunters overlook because they are so engrossed in rubs, scrapes, and trails.

Previous failure is probably the main reason hunters don't seriously attempt to lure in bucks. If it didn't work once, they assume it's a waste of time. Now don't get me wrong. There is no fool-proof lure tactic. However, I know of at least three methods that can bring rutting bucks into range. And one of them comes real close to being perfect, if conditions are right.

THE GRUNT PHENOMENON

I'm going to get the good news over first: Grunting to a mature buck during primary rut is the most reliable buck foolery method mentioned in this chapter. For a bowhunter, it should be considered the next best thing to a surefire tactic. In my opinion, grunting succeeds almost as often as it fails, providing conditions are favorable.

Consider the huge eight-pointer I harvested just a few months before writing this chapter. I had spotted a small buck earlier that morning. Wouldn't you know it: He walked within fifteen yards of my tree stand. I saw the big buck I wanted later, walking a ridge eighty yards to the west. I could tell immediately he wasn't likely to come in my direction.

The peak rut was only days away. This buck was alone. He was also out trooping around two hours after dawn. The wind was blowing from south to north, and my grunt call was handy. The stage was set to try calling this buck in closer.

My first grunt went unheard. The second grunt stopped him. The third prompted him to start walking toward me, and my heart pounded harder with each step he took. He came so rapidly that I wasn't sure there was enough time to prepare for a shooting opportunity. And that's the way it often works. He never stopped coming, and within seconds he was walking by only ten yards away. I released as he passed

The author shot this buck just days before the breeding began after luring him in with a grunt call.
Photo by Vikki L. Trout.

through an opening just before hitting a thicket that would stop a Mack truck, much less my swiftly moving arrow. I won't go into the tracking details that followed, but I will say that eight hours later, my wife, and friend were helping me drag him out.

What's ironic is that just days before taking that buck, I had written a magazine article about grunting to rutting bucks. In that piece, I talked about another buck that was fooled by a grunt call. The conditions were remarkably similar to those that allowed me to take the huge eight-pointer I just mentioned earlier.

Veteran hunters know that whitetails are not vocal animals. Unlike turkeys that converse with other turkeys constantly, and elk that communicate regularly with other elk, deer seldom have much to say. However, they do talk under certain conditions.

Timing is of the essence when calling to a buck. You must call when the bucks are likely to respond, and the rut is the perfect time.

I carry a grunt tube with me throughout the hunting season. That includes the pre-rut and post-rut periods, and the time between. But I know that grunting too early in the season often fails to get a buck's attention, and may even arouse suspicion. Early in the pre-rut period, mature bucks are busy leaving rubs and scrapes but seldom spend any time pursuing does. Small bucks may check out a doe and even try chasing one, but the big boys know the right time is still days or weeks away.

Bucks commonly grunt when they pursue a doe, either while trailing one that passed by a few hours before or when in immediate pursuit of a hot doe. The grunt is triggered by the buck's excitement, so when he hears the grunt of another buck, he may find it necessary to investigate the source.

Not all bucks will respond to a grunt, but the possibility exists that they will when they are not in pursuit of a hot doe. There is little any hunter can do to lure a buck away from a breeding doe, or one that is about to breed.

Random calling is optional. In other words, you can try grunting at various times on stand when you do not see deer. I know some hunters who use a grunt tube every thirty minutes, hoping to attract a customer that is within hearing range. Unfortunately, random calling may hurt more than it helps.

We know a lot about call-shy turkeys, but we still are in the learning stages when it comes to luring in bucks with a grunt tube. Too much calling makes deer suspicious. I agree with that theory, for the most part. Look at it this way: Calling randomly will seldom produce results, and it will alert deer that something is not on the up-and-up. The idea is to grunt to a buck that would not otherwise offer a shooting opportunity. Why risk spoiling an opportunity with random calling?

Grunts may not be heard at a considerable distance. Today, many companies manufacture grunt calls capable of plenty of volume.

VOLUME COUNTS

I can't tell you how many times I have called to a buck, only to have it continue on its merry way because it did not hear my grunts. A gentle breeze, noisy leaves, and calling too softly will cause this. Several years ago, I could not find a grunt tube that provided the volume necessary to attract most of the bucks I saw. Today, there are many that will produce the louder sounds.

It's hard to say just how far away a buck can hear your grunts, but I believe they can easily hear loud grunts more than one hundred yards off when favorable winds exist. By the way, I said "loud" and "favorable." Favorable conditions could mean a buck that is standing still, with no wind and no leaves falling.

But too much volume can hurt when a buck is close in open woods. I seldom grunt to a buck that is only forty to fifty yards away, unless I'm in a dense area. Bucks can hone in on a grunt that they hear loud and clear, and often, if they don't see other deer, they will not come closer.

When calling to a buck, grunt loud enough to get his attention. If he continues onward, you can assume he didn't hear you. Even if a mature buck doesn't want to respond to your call, you can bet he will stop and look toward you. I usually grunt again to help the buck pinpoint the sound, and to make certain he is convinced he did indeed hear a grunt.

Personally, I would much rather carry a loud grunt call. You can always tone it down if necessary, but you can't make a gentle call sound louder.

DO AND DON'T GRUNT WHEN ...

First, never grunt to a downwind buck. He will scent and the game will be over. Normally, when a buck is interested in your grunt, he will come straight at you. Never have I seen one circle and come to a grunt with its nose in the wind. However, if there is any chance that he can wind you, he probably will.

I've already mentioned not grunting to a buck that is in pursuit of a doe. However, having another deer around can be the perfect opportunity

If you have a small buck in the area and spot a big buck at a distance, you have the perfect live decoy to accompany a grunt call.

This buck is trailing another deer. He could be following a doe, or another buck. However, at this moment he's most vulnerable to grunts and will probably respond.

to grunt. The other deer becomes a living decoy that creates a perfect scenario.

Several years ago, I watched a mature buck chase a doe for thirty minutes. Never did the pair pass by in bow range. However, when a button buck walked in and began feeding on acorns nearby, I took advantage of the situation. The bigger buck lost the doe's trail and returned with his nose on the ground. He was about fifty yards from me and close enough to hear my grunt. When he spotted the young buck, he came without hesitation, ears slicked back, ready to kick his rival's you know what. Wow! Did he ever get a surprise when he hit the twenty-yard mark!

Another excellent time to grunt is when you see the right buck trailing another deer. First, consider that you don't know whether he's following a doe, or another buck. Bucks love to follow other bucks during primary rut, almost as much as they love following the trail of a doe.

One of the biggest bucks I ever lured into bow range with a grunt call came to me only after I distracted his attention from the trail of another deer. Unfortunately, I missed that 150-inch buck at twenty-three yards because I rushed the shot. My arrow sailed over his back.

In summarizing the use of grunts calls, let's just say that conditions constitute ninety percent of your success, or failure. You must grunt when everything is right or forget it. Grunt calls work, plain and simple. It's no big deal to pack one along, but it can become a big deal when other tactics fail. Or you could try something else in conjunction with grunts—some of the time.

DECOYING A BUCK

More than likely, you haven't heard much about using decoys to bring "trophy" bucks into range. However, that's not because it's a new tactic that will soon blow all other strategies to the moon and back. Nope. It's just not really a great tactic to depend on. Decoys certainly attract attention, but too many things go wrong, as more and more hunters find out each season.

The primary rut is a great time to decoy bucks, and it's true that decoys today look real convincing. I own a couple of Flambeau decoys that will make you feel *good* if you were to see them from your ambush location. Of course, it's the real deer, particularly the big bucks, we're trying to fool.

Apart from looking real, there's a little more good news about decoys. They can sometimes work wonders and keep a buck from laying low. You know how it is: A buck gets to a field and skirts the edge, sees another deer, or decoy, and just might walk into the middle of an open arena. So much for "safety in numbers."

Another bit of good news is that you can use grunts in conjunction with buck decoys, a tactic that is often quite effective.

Many hunters have wondered which is best—a buck or a doe decoy. However, you can bet that when a mature buck spots a buck decoy and hears a grunt, he probably will want to get in the last word.

It's hard to say which are better, buck or doe decoys, but I'll go with buck decoys during the primary rut. Veteran decoyers might argue the point, but there's nothing carved in stone just yet. I'm fond of buck decoys because I believe they appeal to mature bucks, while little bucks are likely to respond to *any* decoy. Trophy whitetails seldom walk up to every doe they see. They can tell if a doe is breeding, or close to it, and they don't waste their time on just any doe, or decoy. A decoy with small antlers, though, is another story. They just can't ignore another buck during the rut, even if he's small.

The major problem with decoys is those doggoned does. They can't stand to see another deer that doesn't move. Your decoy will drive the does nuts. Even if you use decoys with moveable tails, does may not fall for it. They are curious animals when it comes to strangers in the area. They're also quite inhospitable toward other deer that just stand around and don't do anything.

It's almost inevitable that a doe will see your decoy before a big buck, and when she spots a decoy, she will investigate. Ninety-nine times out of a hundred, that will spoil your chance at a big buck if one happens to be around. Does will stomp, snort, and anything else a deer can do at a decoy to make sure you wasted your day's hunt.

Here are a few suggestions that will increase your chances of success: Wear rubber gloves when handling decoys. Sometimes a doe will walk up and smell a decoy, and you don't want to leave human scent all over the decoy or the surrounding area for that matter. A bowhunter should keep his decoy within range, even if it's on top of him. I would also suggest you take advantage of the first killing opportunity. With a decoy, everything could go wrong without warning. Last but not least, you can use scents to entice a buck to your decoy.

FOOLING BUCKS WITH SCENT

Decoying big bucks is a whole lot newer than using scents to attract them. Still, there's a lot we don't know about using scents, such as which ones work best, and exactly how to use them in ways that are most likely to attract a trophy buck.

I might as well let the cat out of the bag: I'm not a consistent scent user. They do work sometimes, but in my book they rank only one tactic higher up than decoys. I've seen occasional results that have shown me there's a good reason why we have hundreds of scent companies, but that's not to say all scent companies offer proven products.

For best results when it comes to using scent products, you have to understand the different types of scents available. There are commercially manufactured scents and naturals. Some companies have their own deer. Urine is gathered from both bucks and doe, and then bottled and packaged. Sometimes the urine comes from estrous does and becomes one of the company's most "pushed" products.

I don't much favor using cover scents—not even those that smell exactly like the various parts of the environment. They have nothing to do with hunting the different phases of the rut.

That's not to say such manufactured scents are duds. On the contrary, many veteran hunters will attest that they have lured mature bucks into range with synthetics and proudly purchase them as often as they buy genuine scents.

A product's age and packaging might determine if the scent will lure in a big buck, or sanitary conditions could spoil the scent before it's ever packaged. There's a lot we don't know about scents.

From watching captive whitetails hour after hour, I do know that urine is probably the best scent to use. I consistently see bucks lip curl whenever they scent a spot where a doe has urinated. And to be quite honest, it doesn't really matter if that doe is in estrous. If it's early autumn long before the breeding or late winter after the breeding is over, the bucks will usually lip curl.

Just how often a buck will trail the doe that left the scent is questionable. That's hard to determine with captive deer, and impossible in the wild.

Let's assume though, that the sex scent (synthetic, urine or another) is fresh and one hundred percent unspoiled. Whether or not it's going to work for you depends on how you use it, and the mood of the buck that intercepts the scent.

I do know that hot trails are necessary to lure a buck into range. Whenever I make scent trails, I wear boot pads and consistently soak them as I walk. It's expensive, but more effective than soaking the pads once and walking to your ambush location. By soaking them repeatedly, I know the trail gets hotter coming to me. If I soak the pads only once, the trail gets colder with each step taken. Any buck can tell a hot trail from a cold one.

Another method of using scents, and probably one of the best, is to place scent stations around an ambush location. This is most effective for a bowhunter hoping to get a buck to stop, or to force him to come a little closer.

You can use scent pads or cotton containers to make scent stations. Soak each of the stations, hang them about five feet off the ground, sit back, and wait. However, don't expect the bucks to take numbers to see who can get to you first. Scent stations won't draw bucks in from a long distance. As I've discovered enough times, bucks have to be close to the scent to smell it, even when a perfect gentle breeze delivers the smell. Thus, I believe scent stations are most effective once a buck appears.

MOCK SCRAPES

A scent station could become a mock scrape—if you want it to. I've made several over the years, and I've seen several mock scrapes turn into the real thing, worked

Mock scrapes can work, but keep in mind they should be placed in the best possible location to attract a mature buck in daylight hours. *Photo by Fiduccia Enterprises.*

by passing bucks on a regular basis. I have never killed a monster buck over a mock scrape, however.

To make a scrape work, you must first place it in the right location. Some hunters claim that a real scrape or scrapes in the area make a good starting point. However, if there are genuine scrapes, why in the world would you want to take a chance on spoiling them? "Hello!"

That brings us to the starting gate. Always wear rubber boots and rubber gloves when you make a mock scrape. Avoid brushing against debris and continue these practices even when checking mock scrapes in the days ahead.

You'll want to choose a site where there is an overhanging limb. Moreover, you'll want to find a spot where a buck will probably pass by, and that he might come to in daylight hours. This isn't necessarily a well-used trail. Actually, you should already know where the does are spending time, that is where you want your scrape. Also, avoid open areas and place the scrape where it might become a scrape line. In other words, a fenceline, wooded draw or other natural travel corridor might work perfectly.

Scent drippers will keep your mock scrape smelling strong. However, don't handle these devices without using rubber gloves.

As discussed in a previous chapter, scrape lines are much more valuable to the hunter than the biggest, active scrape in the area. Keep that in mind when making a mock scrape. You can make more than one and try to establish a scrape line, or you can make one and hope a buck, or bucks, take care of the others.

Think about your ambush location when preparing a mock scrape. Wind direction and your ability to move in and out of the area without getting too close to the scrape are top priorities.

After selecting a site, use a stick to clear a spot on the ground about three feet in diameter. Don't lay the stick down on the ground and forget it. Carry it with you and stuff into a logjam or something similar, so it won't be found.

Apply scent to the scrape, and don't be shy about turning the bottle upside down. The ground soaks up scent quickly, not to mention rain or even a morning dew day after day. The more scent, the longer it lasts. On the other hand, you might consider using a scent-dripping device—a good way to disperse scent slowly over a long period.

I do believe that a rub nearby might not hurt your chances of a scrape being hit. However, that doesn't necessarily mean it will increase your chances. Choose a tree that a buck will like, such as a maple or pine, remove some bark and step away. You can also apply a tarsal scent to the tree if you really want to be creative.

Hunters use tarsal scent to make a buck think another has moved in. Some hunters claim they are more effective than the hottest sex scents—but the truth is, we'll never know all there is to know about fooling bucks with scents.

In moving on, let me say that I don't believe grunt calls, decoys, and scents are the answer to most problems that haunt the deer hunter. Grunt calls are closest and they can be your ace in the hole, but even they won't substitute for good hunting skills. That's exactly why you should consider these and every other possible method for taking a trophy whitetail when the rutting mechanism dial is turned up all the way. ▨

15
Eye-Level Bucks

Many deer hunters, both archers and gunners, have fallen into a trend. They simply have to hunt from a tree stand. Unfortunately, these individuals are missing fabulous opportunities to get eye-level with a buck. During the primary rut, when vulnerable bucks might cover ground at all hours of the day, the stage is set for taking a trophy whitetail from a ground ambush location, or by still-hunting.

It's been many years since I first nestled into a ground blind. I still remember feeling vulnerable to the sharp eyes of a wary whitetail that approached slowly. However, as the deer walked up to within twenty-five yards, I realized my ground blind had provided the necessary concealment.

At the time, the six-point buck that fell to my charge of black powder was only the second deer I had taken by way of a ground blind. But it did build my confidence, opening the door to many more opportunities. Now don't get me wrong. For four

When ground hunting, don't rely on lots of visibility. The thickest locations are usually best and close encounters are what eye-level contact with a buck is all about. *Photo by Vikki L. Trout.*

decades of hunting whitetails, I have relied on tree stand tactics to fill many of my tags. Nevertheless, I have learned it is advantageous to be versatile, particularly during the primary rut.

Since then, I have taken several whitetails from the ground, including the best buck I've harvested to date. I love the challenge, but even better, I know it increases my chances of success when favorable conditions exist. The conditions I speak of are the ongoing primary rut, and a hunter being in the right place to make it count.

First, consider that nearly every bowhunter and many firearm hunters prefer using tree stands. It has been this way now for eons; if trees are available, most hunters will choose to hunt by way of the perch.

Unfortunately, though, the continued use of tree stands, particularly on lands where intensive hunting pressure occurs, has made the whitetails a bit wiser. No deer walks around consistently looking up, but many whitetails have sharpened their survival instincts by expecting danger from above.

This is the primary reason why many hunters now find it necessary to climb high each time they use tree stands. I can remember using hand-constructed permanent stands years ago and never climbing above twelve feet. I can also remember surprising many deer. But as the years passed and the whitetail became wiser, I found it necessary to climb much higher, and this trend continues today.

Now let's examine those areas that, in order to hunt effectively, require you to stay eye level with the deer. These are prime locations where the dense cover hides the trees. Yet many hunters often sacrifice hunting these great sites simply because they cannot use a tree stand.

There are also times when the hunter is very exposed while hunting from an elevated position. Light camouflage may help you blend against a sky background, but you cannot hide your movements. You can also assume that a deer may see your silhouette.

Once the leaves have fallen, which is usually the case during the primary rut, I find it much easier to remain hidden by getting eye level with the bucks. If done correctly, a ground blind can totally conceal me from the sharp eyes of the wariest doe and the trophy buck that might accompany her.

Now for the big reason why you should consider staying eye level with the bucks during the primary rut: You can hunt most anywhere, and you can make things happen. You are never stuck in a lull zone. Moving to new ambush locations, or still-hunting when favorable conditions exist, are proven and dependable tactics for killing a big buck. But you need to know how to do it right.

CHOOSING THE AMBUSH SITE

To begin, whether you're a bow or a gun hunters, don't choose a location where visibility allows you to see for a considerable distance and shoot farther. A ground blind located smack-dab in the middle of a thicket, where visibility is poor, can often be a better choice.

Keep in mind, mature bucks often prefer the thickest cover to travel in daylight hours. The good news, though, is that you are better hidden in these locations, too. Thus, when choosing your ambush location, disregard visibility. Have faith that the deer will soon show up where you want them, and be assured that if they do, you will get a shot within easy range. Just because I use a firearm, for example, I do not mind setting up in an area of poor visibility where I can see only thirty to forty yards to the right trail, scrape or food source. And when bowhunting on the ground, I often find myself selecting an ambush site only twenty yards from where the deer will soon be.

HIDING OUT

With modern camouflage, it is not difficult to blend in with any surroundings. In fact it's probably easier when hunting on the ground than from a tree.

Today's commercial blinds have opened the door to lots of opportunities, but the ground hunting tactics herein are focused on natural setups—using the terrain and foliage for concealment. Commercial ground blinds are effective, particularly those that are placed ahead of time so deer get used to them. However, many times you must select a ground location immediately, and nothing beats a natural look to keep you hidden.

I almost always avoid setting up on top of hills, where a thick background does not come easily. Instead, I will select the side of a hill where there is no daylight behind me. When hunting in flat country, I rely totally on my constructed ground blind itself to conceal me.

The author has taken a number of whitetails while hunting from the ground relying upon natural foliage for concealment. *Photo by Vikki L. Trout.*

I prefer to pile up natural foliage behind me—limbs and vegetation, and/or trees when available. However, I do not limit the construction of the blind to my backside. I will place the debris on both sides to help me remain hidden in case a deer approaches from an unexpected direction.

As for the front side, where the shot is likely to occur, I have found that having a tree—or trees—to hide behind works best. Only recently, I cashed in on a whitetail while bowhunting on the ground by getting behind a fairly small pine tree. My background had enough natural foliage to help me blend effectively. Finally, I also attribute my success to hunting on a suitable day when the wind direction was stable.

A tree-stand hunter will sometimes go undetected by an approaching deer, even when an air current shifts directions briefly in favor of the whitetail. The ground hunter, though, is rarely forgiven. The wrong wind direction will most certainly give the hunter away without warning, and his or her hunt will end in disaster. For this reason, I suggest that you never take chances and settle into the ambush location only when you know the wind is favorable for you.

MAKE THE FIRST SHOT COUNT

When hunting an eye-level buck, you might be tempted to take your shot before the deer has become broadside or quartered away. However, it is vitally important, particularly for the bowhunter, that you wait for the best shooting opportunity. The firearm hunter can also discover quickly that a quartering-into shot is unwarranted.

You should always carry along pruning shears or a small hand saw to open shooting lanes. This is as helpful for the gun hunter as it is for the bowhunter. When clearing is necessary, and it usually is if you have selected the best and thickest location, do it first with your eyes from the shooting angle. Trim only what is necessary, and then return to the blind and look for other limbs before clearing more, since it's always

When clearing shooting lanes for hunting on the ground, it's better to clear too little than too much.

better not to remove too much. Believe me, if there's one thing a whitetail will spot quickly, it is a thick area that has suddenly opened up.

Finally, use a small stool to keep yourself lower to the ground and better hidden when the time comes to raise your bow or gun. One exception is when you choose a spur-of-the-moment setup behind a clump of thick trees. Then you will probably blend better if you stand.

Sitting keeps me more comfortable for longer periods and helps me avoid unnecessary moving. Also, most of us can shoot more accurately when sitting. When bowhunting, it's much easier to master shooting from a seat than it is to try getting off the ground and onto your knees.

If you've never tried hunting from a ground blind, the primary rut is a good time to begin. It's yesterday's technique, and something that can fool a trophy buck when he's most vulnerable. But that's not all. It makes still-hunting an option when favorable conditions exist.

INTRODUCTION TO STILL-HUNTING

I've mentioned Tim Hillsmeyer and some of his hunting tactics previously in this book, and for good reason. He has certainly tagged his share of mature bucks with bow and gun. However, there's more to his story. He started bowhunting in the late 1960s, and in those early years, he never climbed into a tree stand. He relied solely on still-hunting to outsmart a few of the bucks that roamed the countryside near his southern Indiana home.

Eventually, Hillsmeyer did begin hunting by way of the tree stand, but only after years of experience hunting on the ground. He learned that the still-hunter must wait for the best days. He also learned that some days are just made for the stalker. That's exactly why he still hunts on the ground occasionally.

Hillsmeyer's closest shot from the ground occurred in 1985, when he shot a 125-inch buck at only three yards. Success did not come easy, however, and he refers to his early years of still-hunting as the "School of Hard Knocks." It was simply trial and error until he gained the necessary confidence to be a successful still-hunter.

Tim Hillsmeyer shot this 125-inch buck at a distance of only three yards while still-hunting.

WHY STILL-HUNT?

"If you limit yourself to only one style of hunting, you're going to be limited on the number of opportunities you will get to be successful," explained Hillsmeyer. "I would never go fishing with only one lure, nor would I want to hunt by using only one tactic. On some days you may need to still-hunt to see deer."

Still-hunting can sharpen your overall woodsmanship skills. It may be that you will learn more about patterning bucks simply because you must meet them on their terms. Hillsmeyer still-hunts during all phases of the rut and relies much on what he learns that way to pattern big bucks. Remember, during the primary rut you can often count on bucks to move, which increases your chances of succeeding.

Hillsmeyer compares stalking bucks to squirrel hunting. Most squirrel hunters see deer up close, but often refuse to try hunting on the ground when the deer season opens. Squirrel hunting forces you to slow down, one of the necessary skills for being a successful stalker. Hillsmeyer recalled reading an article many years ago in which a bowhunter stated, "If you think you're moving too slow, then slow down." This statement has helped Hillsmeyer considerably. In other words, it's not how much ground you cover, it's how cover it.

STILL-HUNTING TACTICS

The hunter must know the area to still-hunt it effectively. However, Hillsmeyer said that you are sure to learn the terrain better after still-hunting any area a few times. Practice makes perfect.

You will move from one type of terrain to the other when still-hunting, starting in a wooded area, perhaps, and moving into a thicket or grown-up field. A universal camo will help you blend with a variety of terrain.

A quality binocular is essential, but it must not hinder you when it comes time to shoot. Hillsmeyer puts the strap over his right shoulder and places the binocular under his left arm to keep it out of his way.

Hillsmeyer also recommends dressing lighter than normal in colder temperatures. Too many clothes, he claims, will usually hurt

Still-hunting is more in your favor after a rain and/or when conditions are breezy. However, it's how you go about it that will determine your chance of success when stalking a mature buck.

146

more than they help. Sweating comes all too quickly when you still-hunt, and you must be able to shoot comfortably without your clothing interfering with your equipment.

Veteran still-hunters prefer to do it after a rain, when they can move quietly. Hillsmeyer also likes stalking under these conditions, but he stays on the ground other times, too. A breezy day sets up another opportunity. Even a gentle wind will help to deaden the sounds of a moving hunter, but be warned: The stalker must watch every step.

"I always look ahead whenever I stop to see where I should place my feet," noted Hillsmeyer. "You have to avoid any debris that will create a disturbance. If you can do this, you don't have to wait for a wet and windy day to still-hunt."

When the primary rut begins, Hillsmeyer said that the bucks begin moving on alternate routes looking for does. Once a doe in the area has come into estrous, it may cause the trophy bucks to make mistakes. These bucks will cover more ground, giving the stalker a chance to intercept them.

Although most stalkers might prefer walking with the wind in their faces, Hillsmeyer often moves into a crosswind when trying to locate a big buck.

"I have seldom seen big bucks walking with the wind at their tail," he says. "They just don't make these kinds of mistakes often."

By walking into a crosswind, Hillsmeyer can often spot the bucks doing the same. And if his human scent goes undetected, it all boils down to seeing the buck before it sees you. That's the key to shifting the hunt more in favor of the hunter.

According to Hillsmeyer, every hunter has a sixth sense that can become an accurate, reliable tool. It tells you when you should stop and when you should move. Also, look for vantage points whenever you stop, simply because you never know when a shot opportunity will come. The stalker must always believe that a buck may be close anytime and place.

As Hillsmeyer puts it, "Ground hunting is an exciting opportunity to play the game in the whitetail's field." He's right. You're in their element and you must pass a difficult test to be successful. When you do, you will experience the thrill of winning against the odds.

Keep in mind, many of the tactics mentioned in this chapter, and others in Section II, cannot be relied upon when hunting pressure intensifies. And let's face it; at some point during the primary rut, pressure will turn any hot area into a dead-zone without warning. ▪

16
High-Anxiety Bucks

At some point during the primary rut the bucks in your area will undoubtedly become severely stressed due to hunting pressure, compliments of you and me. It comes without warning and it's an annual event that can't be escaped.

Hunting pressure affects does, fawns, and subordinate bucks just as it does mature bucks, so how will it your hunting during the primary rut? For starters, you already know that your best chance of ambushing a trophy deer is to be where the does are hanging out. If the does are there, the bucks will come. The kicker is, if the does are no longer visiting the same food sources and bedding areas they once

Hunting pressure affects the does just as it does the bucks. Their food sources and bedding areas will change without warning.

did, you can forget about the bucks showing up. Of course, there's a little more to the story, as we've already discussed, but you get the point. More than likely the hunting pressure had already led to high-anxiety bucks in your area before the does were affected.

Just how long it takes for the bucks to feel pressure and change their habits depends upon the size of the area and how many hunters are there. Even a two hundred-acre area can change overnight, as I've experienced on more than one occasion. The smaller the area, the fewer hunters it takes to send a message that immediately causes deer to change their movements. In fact, just one hunter can change it all.

It's not only firearm hunters that send bucks into a nervous frenzy. I know of one wildlife refuge that allows bowhunting by random draw only. Even during the primary rut, the place goes sour in just a couple of days once a handful of archers are turned loose.

The changing habits of a buck will vary, but two facts stand out: Even a little hunting pressure will cause a buck to change bedding areas, and the more pressure he endures, the more nocturnal he becomes.

I won't say much about nocturnal bucks in this chapter, except that I don't believe any buck ever becomes totally nocturnal. It might seem like he has, but chances are he's just not where you thought he should be. Also, during the primary rut, the bucks maintain a breeding instinct. Although their survival instincts might outweigh their breeding instincts, the urge to breed is still a factor. However, by the post-rut period and any time scars of the previous hunting pressure are very pronounced, a mature buck might move less in daylight hours than he ever did before. You'll get to read about so-called nocturnal bucks in Part III.

REMAIN CONFIDENT

Enough said about the difficulty of hunting pressured bucks. I don't want to completely shake your confidence for hunting the rut once the pressure sets in. Confidence provides hope for tagging a pressured trophy whitetail.

We often hear a lot of shooting on opening morning, and our gut feeling is that the buck we are hunting has surely fallen to someone else. That's always a possibility, but it's equally likely he's still out there. Consider that many hunters will be happy enough to take any legal buck or doe, and a lot of the shooting could be from meat hunters. It's important for you to believe that the trophy buck on which you've pinned your hopes is still a candidate for your attention.

It's no big secret that most deer are harvested during the first two or three days of the firearm season, if not on opening day. Knowing this, hunters are eager to get out there sooner rather than later—recognizing that once bucks get pressured, they will start disappearing, and the biggest, oldest, wisest bucks are the first to take cover.

Even though hunting pressure might cause a mature buck to move less in daylight hours, he will still maintain breeding instincts.

It's also true that during the breeding season, a doe might help you by leading the right buck past your stand. But overall, a buck's survival instincts suddenly become more powerful than his urge to breed. They do remain killable, though, because they don't actually crawl into a hole and disappear.

Confidence will keep you in the woods, and staying there is absolutely necessary to kill a pressured buck. You won't see as many deer as you do at other times, but keep in mind the big bucks are more prone to making mistakes. You only need to know where they will be to take advantage of their errors.

NO-MAN'S LAND

Big bucks head for no-man's land once the hunting pressure intensifies. However, allow me to set the record straight. You might think no-man's land is some place miles from anywhere, perhaps someplace that you can only get in to using your luckiest parachute. Nope. No-man's land is probably close to your hunting area, and could be smack-dab in the middle of it.

Granted, you do have to get away from the crowds. You see, no matter how well you go about reducing your scent and taking all the other precautions necessary to keep your presence unknown, some other hunter could be screwing up the area as soon as you walk to or from your ambush location. This is precisely why I have a problem hunting with certain outfitters, who try to run through too many hunters, allowing the area to be spoiled. When hunting big bucks, I must be in control; when I'm not in control, who's to say what's going on? I can hunt a great ambush location, but the outfitter might send in Crazy Joe, who decides he's going to hike around the area for twenty minutes. So much for that hotspot.

Typically, no-man's land is an area where man doesn't venture. It could be a square tract of no more than one hundred yards, or a narrow strip thirty yards wide and two hundred yards long. And it could be anywhere, including in your own backyard.

Be prepared to change to a new ambush location at a moment's notice. In many areas, including some private lands, hunting pressure will force bucks into different habits only twenty-four to forty-eight hours after the firearm season debuts.

HIDEAWAYS

Common sense tells us that bucks seek security in out-of-the-way places. In my early days of hunting, I considered these areas to be places where the devil himself wouldn't go. As the years passed, though, and I remained persistent, always looking for pressured bucks, it became obvious the bucks were right under my nose.

Bucks like it thick, and any dense area appears attractive to them when they're pressured. Bucks look for various types of hideaways, including pine thickets, stands of bramble bushes, cutover areas, honeysuckle and saplings. If the area looks to you like it would be difficult to get in and out of, it is probably an ideal place for a pressured buck.

Of course, not every area has an appropriate thicket. Be aware that a mature buck, and particularly does and fawns, will not leave an area and travel miles to get away from pressure. They stick around and hide in whatever is available.

Now that I told you about dense areas appealing to big bucks, you should know there's a flip-side to everything. Surprisingly, overgrown weed fields usually attract high-anxiety bucks, yet most hunters overlook them and seek denser areas. This is precisely why a buck will not hesitate to seek out a bedding area in nothing more than a grown-up field.

Many landowners take advantage of set-aside programs, leaving their fields to grow. By late autumn, at the onset of the hunting pressure, these fields are often waist-deep and very attractive to a nervous whitetail.

Then there are wetlands. A friend of mine set up a stand in a swamp after being drawn for a special hunt. He assumed most hunters would not penetrate the marsh, and instead would stick to the timber and thickets surrounding the wetland. On the second day of his hunt, after seeing several deer, he cashed in on a huge buck. Although most hunters participating in the hunt claimed they saw nothing but other hunters, the successful hunter said he did not see anyone.

Although bucks will bed in lightly flooded areas, they do not bed down in deep standing water. However, they go into these places because they know hunters don't. The bucks utilize the water as a safe haven, and seek out dry land in the middle of the wetlands.

I know of one hunting group that leases land in a low area. Each year, about the time the primary rut is in full swing and the hunting pressure is intensifying, the

When the wisest old bucks move to escape hunting pressure, you must also move. Try setting up on the perimeters of grown-up fields, standing corn, cutover areas, and swampy ground.

area usually floods. The deer head for a ridge in the middle of the flooded terrain and stay there, enjoying security at its finest. There are usually an ample supply of acorns on the ridge to keep the deer fed. Hunters have been quite successful taking a boat into the area and setting up along the perimeter of the ridge.

Standing corn is another option. True, there is little chance of finding standing corn by the time the rut arrives, but it's not impossible. Sometimes, a farmer harvests everything except a small patch of corn, and even that small area can become a haven for a spooky buck.

NARROWING THE FIELD

You must locate the best possible hideaway or hideaways in your area. That's not easy on any day, but it's even more difficult when the bucks are pressured and you have to start scouting all over again.

I suggest you walk the perimeters of areas that might attract a pressured buck and look for rubs and scrapes. Despite a big buck's desire to hide out, something in his old head keeps him thinking about pretty little does. Thus, the first thing he will want to do when he exits his hideaway is leave sign. For him, it's probably a territorial factor to mark the new area with scent.

You should also look for trails with fresh sign and droppings. Don't look for wide, gouged trails; any trails you locate have probably not been used long. In some cases, you might only find tracks. The key is to hone in on anything that points to a possible hideaway.

STAKE 'EM OUT

Once you have located a promising hideout, you are one step closer to filling a tag. Now you have to decide how to hunt the hideaway, and the better you know the area, the easier it will be to select the right ambush locations.

When choosing an ambush location, you must avoid penetrating the hideaway. This is a buck's sacred ground. He's already been pushed there, and even if it took a sound dose of hunting pressure to do it, it will take only a little more of the same to sound the alarm and push him to another hideout.

During the firearm season, I rely on bowhunting methods, and I don't worry about visibility, even when hunting grown-up fields and marshes. I look at it this way: A buck selects a hideout because it makes him feel protected. Once he moves, he will probably head wherever there's cover to keep him secluded. Thus, the best setup is probably on the fringe of the hideout, near the thickest cover that borders it.

Consider that any encounter with a hiding buck will probably be a close encounter. A mature buck is cautious and not as likely to make the same mistake he might have made on opening day of the firearm season. You can bet your luckiest tree stand that he will not move with the wind at his south end. In other words, if the wind is out of the north and you set up on the south end of a thicket because your scent blows directly away from the buck's hideaway, you probably won't see much.

Then again, a cautious buck in hiding will travel crosswind, or with the wind in his face. You can't set up with the wind blowing directly into the buck's nose, but you can plan your ambush for a crosswind.

Selecting several ambush sites will keep you versatile and keep the bucks guessing. Tree-stand hunters can never rely on only one ambush location, since the wind will not be right all the time. However, don't allow yourself to slip back in time and start hunting well-used trails that once attracted the does.

Each year there are hunters who bring their bucks out of the woods late in the breeding season simply because they did *something right.* Most of them understood the options and remained confident. They knew ahead of time where a pressured buck would hang out, and that any area could be considered a safe haven year after year. Thus, if you find a reliable area one season and you don't get your buck before the pressure accelerates, remember it for next time.

I'm not going to kid you. It's tough killing a pressured buck even during the rut, and no matter how much you know about their changing habits, you might as well be ready for a challenge. Here's the way it works: Within twenty-four hours, you can go from the easiest conditions for ambushing a mature buck to the most difficult. ▪

17
Tracking a Rutting Buck

W aiting for the right buck to come along is what trophy hunting is all about. Sometimes it takes weeks—sometimes it takes years. When the perfect shot opportunity finally arrives, though, the last thing you want is to blow it by hitting the deer poorly. Nevertheless, tracking a wounded animal is as common as tree stands in the deer woods. Anyone who hunts often is going to find himself tracking his own deer, or helping someone else track one.

But tracking a buck in the primary rut is not the same as tracking a buck during the pre-rut and post-rut periods. It's a completely different game, and knowing the differences could help you recover the trophy of a lifetime.

In my book *Finding Wounded Deer,* I briefly discussed tracking a wounded buck during the rut. Of course, it will only be necessary if you don't hit him perfectly. We can start there.

Assuming you already have an understanding of shot placement, you already know that a buck hit in both lungs won't run far. A broadhead or projectile will get the job done effectively and promptly when it passes through the vital organs. However, less than perfect hits will result in a tracking experience you may never forget. None of us knows all there is to know about tracking a wounded deer. But you should have a complete understanding of the key facts, including the common habits of a wounded buck during the rut, before circumstances lead you to the task of tracking a rutting one.

COLORS OF BLOOD

Some blood is bright red and some is dark. Both shades tell different stories, and either could mean a long tracking situation. Lung shots result in bright red blood—sometimes pink. Heart and artery shots produce crimson blood, but it's never dark. These wounds result in a downed deer fairly quickly and a short tracking job. Little or no experience is usually necessary.

However, bright blood can also indicate a muscle wound, and dark blood means a wound to the paunch. Either way, you face the possibility of a long tracking situation.

Before assuming what a wounded rutting buck might do next, you must first know what type of wound you are dealing with. *Photo by Vikki L. Trout.*

Many veteran hunters can recognize the difference in the colors of blood at first glance. It's easier to do when the blood is wet, since dried blood tends to look dark. Blood color is also easiest to determine when there is lots of it. Keep in mind, though, you might find both bright and dark blood when you shoot at a deer that quarters into or away. For instance, a projectile could enter in the paunch and exit through the hip if the animal was quartering into when you shot. Quartering-into shots are not recommended, but I say this to point out how easily you can be fooled if your broadhead or bullet angles through the animal.

WHAT'S NEXT?

I would suggest you never begin tracking a deer unless you know the type of wound you are dealing with, since some require waiting—and some don't. Normally, I base it upon the color of blood alone, but if dark blood prevails, I know the wound is to the liver, stomach and/or intestines, and it's best to wait. If I find bright blood, I pursue the animal quickly and quietly.

Many muscle wounds are superficial. However, some of these deer are recovered when pushed slowly and quietly to keep them bleeding. A paunch shot deer, on the other hand, should be left alone for several hours. I usually allow four to six hours to begin tracking, and sometimes I wait overnight if I shoot the deer in the evening. Most gut-shot deer will bed down quickly (that includes big bucks during rut). Because of a sparse blood trail, it's best to let the animal alone. Time is then on your side. Always remember the golden rule that applies to tracking a wounded deer anytime: The less distance you have to track the animal, the better your chance of a recovery.

READING A BLOOD TRAIL

You can learn a lot by following a blood trail. For instance, if drops of blood are shaped like teardrops, you can assume the deer is running. The splatter marks are usually found only at the top of the droplet, pointing out which way the deer is traveling.

A standing or walking deer will leave round drops of blood. Usually, there are splatter marks completely encircling the droplet. If the deer is walking, the blood droplets may be spaced a few inches or more apart, but if the deer stands in one place, the blood will accumulate in small areas and might appear as pools.

That brings us to another important fact: Never assume a deer is about to go down just because you find lots of blood. True, artery wounds will usually result in a large quantity of blood and a deer succumbing in seconds, and internal bleeding kills far more deer than external bleeding. But external bleeding can fool you. Consider that a deer must lose one-third of its blood to bleed to death. Now consider how much just one cup of blood would spread over an area, though it isn't

The author's son John attempts to decipher the wound he is dealing with. The better you can read a blood trail, the better understanding you will have about how to track a rutting buck.

even close to one-third of the volume of blood in an adult deer's body.

Two blood trails usually tell you that a deer is bleeding on both sides, and that there are both entry and exit holes. That's good news because more penetration is always better, and it results in more blood getting to the ground.

Gut-shot deer seldom bleed a lot externally. Typically, stomach and intestinal matter will often clog the departure and sometimes the entry hole, particularly once a deer travels a distance of fifty to one hundred yards. Blood might get to the ground at first, but it will quickly dissipate. By the way, you should know that any wound to the paunch will result in a dead deer, usually within a few hours. Deer with intestinal wounds often go farther and don't succumb as quickly as those with liver and stomach wounds.

Muscle wounds often bleed profusely, but many of them will often clot after the animal travels one hundred to two hundred yards. Shoulder and back wounds typically clot faster than neck, leg, and hip wounds. Hip wounds seldom clot totally, which allows the hunter to stay on the trail of the animal, and most hunters recover a hip-shot deer if they pursue it slowly and quietly.

BIG BUCK ENDURANCE

The distance you must track a deer in order to recover it depends upon several factors, a few of which I've already mentioned. However, when it comes to bucks in the primary rut, some of the "golden rules" change.

For instance, most double-lung shot deer will run no more than eighty to one hundred yards before going down, if they don't drop immediately. Big bucks seem to travel farther. I know of one that didn't go down until he surpassed the 175-yard marker—a mature buck that field dressed over 250 pounds. Not all, but many other big bucks I've observed and heard about, showed similar stamina on their final run.

For many years, I kept statistics on the distances deer ran with different types of wounds. These records included bucks, does, and fawns. In nearly every situation, mature bucks ran greater distances than does and young bucks. Not surprisingly, fawns usually succumbed faster than bucks and does: Most adult deer hit through both lungs traveled eighty to one hundred yards before dropping. Most fawns traveled less than sixty yards.

I can still recall a buck I shot one morning during the primary rut. The liver was hit, and in most cases this results in a dead deer within two to three hours. Not this time. I started tracking the huge eleven-pointer at noon, several hours after shooting him. A couple of hours later I lost the blood trail, and at 3 P.M., jumped the buck from his bed. I marked the spot and left the deer alone.

The following morning I returned with Vikki and Tim Hillsmeyer. After about two hours, we located the buck. He had covered a distance of several hundred yards from where I shot him. Stomach tissue had clogged both the entry and departure holes made by my arrow, which prevented blood from getting to the ground. Upon field dressing the deer, I found a perfect slice in the liver where the broadhead had passed through. Based upon the time I shot him and the time I jumped him, the buck had positively survived the liver wound for at least nine hours. The actual time he survived could have been much longer.

None of this means too much as far as a recovery is concerned. A perfect hit is a downed animal. Even the big bucks that travel a few extra yards usually leave easy-to-follow blood trails when hit well. What's important, though, is that in the case of a less-than-perfect shot, a buck can travel farther than most deer would with a similar wound.

HOME RANGE OF RUTTING BUCKS

Previously in this book, I discussed home ranges and distances a buck might travel in the rut. Not all mature bucks will travel long distances during the primary rut, but many do, and almost all will go beyond the home range where they spent most of their time during the pre-rut period.

It's normal for wounded deer to circle if they don't succumb quickly. Deer with muscle wounds, as well as most paunch-shot deer, might travel for a short distance, but after one hundred to two hundred yards, most will make a gradual turn and start angling. They do not move in straight lines.

The exception is a big buck during the primary rut. I've noticed they travel a near straight line, and you can usually figure that's what they'll do when pushed. I speculate that this is because, when wounded, they prefer the sense of security they had in their home range, perhaps the familiarity of their old bedding grounds. There is no concrete evidence to explain why most wounded rutting bucks travel farther than most wounded does, or farther than bucks do during pre-rut and post-rut. However, you can bet they will—providing they don't die before given the opportunity.

Earlier in this chapter, I discussed paunch-shot deer bedding down. I don't believe that a gut-shot buck will want to travel too far before bedding down just because he happens to be outside his home range. Whether it's the primary rut or the pre-rut, bucks with abdominal wounds seem to bed down just as soon as they feel safe. The difference I've seen is when a buck receives a muscle or abdominal wound, and is pushed. I've pushed both bucks and does during pre-rut and post-rut, and they typically circle and do not travel straight for any considerable distance. But during the primary rut, the bucks will cover more ground and stay on a straighter course.

The distances I have tracked wounded bucks during the rut have varied, and I have followed bucks just as far in the pre-rut as in the post-rut, but they didn't really

Most wounded deer tend to circle after traveling a few hundred yards. During the primary rut, many bucks tend to travel straight for long distances.

During the primary rut, bucks often travel a considerable distance from their home range. Could it be they attempt to head for their familiar stomping grounds when wounded?

end up anywhere different. In other words, during the primary rut they traveled nearly a straight line and ended up in strange territory a mile or more from where they were shot. Early and late in the season, when I suspect bucks are in their home range, I have also tracked them for a mile, but they did not end up more than a quarter- or half-mile from where they were shot.

For more detailed tracking facts, you should find yourself a reliable tracking book. Remember: If you have to track a wounded mature buck during the primary rut, expect a few surprises. As for tracking post-rut bucks, it's back to the same old stuff—well almost. Please read on. ■

The Post Rut

18
Beating the Odds

The post-rut period provides many opportunities to kill big bucks. A late firearm season, blackpowder hunt, or archery season is an option in most states and provinces. Some hunters claim winter is the best time to take a super buck. I don't agree with that, but I do believe you can beat the odds easier than you think.

There are plenty of ways to increase your chances of killing a mature buck, such as paying attention to foods that deer can't live without and hunting during the second rut. So let's start with the most pressing question: How can you beat the odds and kill a buck near his bedding area just after the end of the primary rut?

The primary breeding cycle is typically short-lived, usually about two to three weeks, and only a few days during that time are extremely hot. The post-rut period begins as soon as the breeding ends and continues until the hunting seasons wrap up.

The author does not believe any buck ever becomes totally nocturnal. However, they do limit their daytime movements considerably with the arrival of the post-rut period.

Many hunters have gotten the idea that once the rut is over, the surviving bucks become nocturnal and there is little or no chance of tagging a trophy. That is partially correct. The chances of killing a big buck are slimmer, but not because the bucks have become nocturnal. One reason there is little chance of shooting a wall hanger is that most individuals give up and don't hunt again until the following autumn. You can't kill one if you're not out there.

Going into the post-rut season, you should realize that some bucks always survive the earlier firearm and archery seasons, and that includes mature bucks. Some areas have more survivors than others, but even in areas where the worst odds of survival exist, you can bet that somewhere not far from your favorite ambush location there's a big buck tucked away in a thicket that you never knew existed.

Now, getting back to the nocturnal theory, it's no big secret that whitetails move more at night, preferring to lie up in daylight hours. But since hunters enjoy much of our success in early morning and late afternoon, thirty minutes from the dark hours, it's obvious that deer are not completely nocturnal by nature.

During the post-rut, it might seem that the oldest, smartest bucks become totally nocturnal, yet nothing could be further from the truth. They may be moving less in daylight than they did when hot does were flashing in front of their eyes, but the bucks don't crawl in a hole and stay there waiting for next year's primary rut.

Hunting pressure is the one big reason bucks appear to be nocturnal. They have

Hunting close to bedding areas might be the best post-rut tactic, but only until the bucks calm down.

It's hard determining a big buck exists during post-rut. Even a subordinate buck such as this one could leave big tracks. The author suggests you assume that any area might be home to a mature buck in late season. *Photo by Ted Rose.*

been bumped, cursed, and ambushed by deer hunters for many weeks. A wise and mature buck probably hits an anxiety peak, reaching a point that he will take no more chances. Instinctively, he only thinks of ways to survive, and that includes lying up and moving less.

Unlike the primary rut, when their constant movement gives us ample opportunities to locate and kill them, you won't see bucks often in post-rut, if at all, because they are no longer traveling in search of does. Let's not forget: More often than not, we tag trophies because they did something wrong—not because we did something right.

Now consider bedding areas. During the post-rut period, bucks will spend more time wherever they feel safe and secure. Some bedding areas are quite dependable and will attract the same buck day after day, which is similar to the habits of big bucks during the pre-rut period. Their bedding areas may change with the environment, such as when a food source dries up, but they prefer spending time in the same old safe haven.

You should also consider the home range of a mature buck. During the primary rut, it might or might not be close to where you see him, but it will be close to where you saw him during the pre-rut. In other words, probably due to a buck returning to his home range after the breeding ends, it's no surprise to spot the same buck in post-rut that you see during pre-rut. It's true, though, that plenty of bucks don't make it back to their home range in post-rut. Some are hanging around a wall somewhere instead.

While I have seen bucks in both the post-rut and pre-rut periods over the years, it's not something I can count on. Because a buck's home range might be large, and some just don't survive, the possibility of seeing a certain deer again, months after seeing them the first time, is not good. But it does happen.

The best way to see a buck in his home range during the early post-rut, or to intercept a trophy you never knew was there, is to hunt bedding areas. That's not easy, and it takes lots of caution and patience, but it can be done successfully.

Keep in mind, the foliage will have changed considerably from the pre-rut days of autumn and, in most cases, it will have changed some since the primary rut— just days or weeks earlier. More leaves have fallen, knee-high foliage in the woods is now hardly noticeable, and even tall weed fields look distraught. In other words, areas that once provided dense cover have turned into open places that would make an antelope happy to roam.

Fortunately, there are areas that will attract mature bucks looking for something to hide in. Cutover areas, honeysuckle thickets, grown-up fencelines and briar patches, as well as pine and cedar groves, are all popular bedding areas. Open hardwoods are at the bottom of the list.

And now for the good news. It doesn't take a large bedding area to make a big buck happy.

I can still remember one Indiana buck that shocked me several years ago—and more than once. I first spotted him leaving an encirclement of fallen logs one evening about twenty minutes before dusk. I was hunting near a field and trail when I saw the huge deer walking away from the fifty-yard area of downed timber. I had just looked that way moments before and seen nothing. My tree stand was set up about eighty yards away and I had a birds-eye view, so I know the buck hadn't come from anywhere else. Nope! He obviously had been in the logjam when I came to my stand that afternoon, and I knew I had been lucky to reach my stand without bumping him. I sat with my bow in hand that evening and watched intently as the 140-inch buck walked a fenceline and disappeared into a nearby shallow woods.

Now for the real kicker: I returned to the same stand two days later, fired up just knowing the buck was in the area. However, when I was within fifteen yards of my stand, I heard something, looked up, and saw him leaving the same logjam. Unfortunately, he left in a hurry. He had obviously spotted me approaching.

I never saw that buck again, but I probably got what I deserved. I should have known he might bed again in the same thicket, but I didn't get the message. Instead, I chose to hunt the field and did not consider the buck might be on top of me.

I'm sure you get the point. Nice big thick areas are attractive to all deer in winter, but it doesn't take a big area to satisfy a big buck. If he can walk into

When searching for late-season bedding areas, do so carefully and avoid getting too close to areas that could potentially attract a mature buck. The best way to determine if a buck is using the area is to set up and hope he shows.

something and disappear, a buck is happy. That is, until someone like you or I comes along and bumps him.

Anytime you are looking for post-rut bedding areas, do so cautiously. Big bucks are always on edge, but by the time the primary rut is over, they are at the breaking point. Don't approach bedding areas too closely. You never know if they are getting used with any consistency until you hunt near them a few times when the wind is favorable, but that's precisely the best way to determine if the right customer is hanging around. Even then, it could be you won't see a big buck if he is there. You should be sure about that, though, before moving on.

A couple of years ago, my wife and I hunted the late season hard in Illinois, but we were not seeing any respectable bucks. I remembered one area of dense bramble bushes only about one-fourth mile from where we had set up stands, and one afternoon when the wind was favorable, I planned a ground hunt near the small thicket, mainly to keep an eye on it and see "what" might be utilizing it. The afternoon's hunt ended abruptly. I was within sixty yards of the thicket when two big bruisers came busting out of the briars.

That brings up another point about bedding areas: It seems mature bucks don't want to share. I've noticed that some bedding areas attract does, fawns, and subordinate bucks, while others seem to appeal to mature bucks only. I don't believe that the type of bedding area has anything to do with that, however. More likely, big bucks just like having an area to themselves.

Finding the right ambush location is never easy near bedding areas. The biggest mistake, as I've already pointed out, is getting too close. Bedding areas in winter are usually thin, which leads to disaster for an approaching hunter. Some hunters might claim they located big tracks and assumed a big buck was using an area, but that theory just doesn't hold up. Big-antlered bucks might or might not leave big tracks, and the same applies to small-antlered bucks. During the post-rut period, it's never easy determining that a big buck is in the area, unless you see him.

I suggest you stay seventy-five to one hundred yards away from any bedding area, and be there only when the wind is positively in your favor. I'm not so sure

Bucks like it thick any time. However, in post-rut, when the foliage is limited, a deer will select even the smallest thicket. Never overlook any area that is big enough to hide a mature buck.

that you can expect a big buck to come walking out of there with the wind at his south end, but he won't mind walking into a crosswind.

Equally important, arrive early in the morning and stay until legal shooting time ends in the evening. That's the normal tactic of stand hunting anytime in deer season, but it's at the top of the ambush tactics list in post-rut. As I said previously, no buck is totally nocturnal. However, you can bet that the best times for spotting a wise old buck will be right at dawn and at dusk.

One more thought about hunting the evenings in post-rut. When hunting near bedding areas, it's more common to hear a deer walking than to see one. They move late, slowly and cautiously. I know of one that got to the edge of a bedding area about ten minutes before dusk. He stood there motionless and stared into the woods until darkness arrived. Then he left the bedding area and moved past me—staying out of range.

Hunting on top of a bedding area often means staying in your ground blind or tree stand until the owls leave home. If you suspect a deer is on the move near you at dusk, I would suggest you wait until you know he's gone before leaving the area. Remaining undetected is absolutely necessary if you hope to ambush a big buck near the same spot on another evening.

Hunting a bedding area is a primary tactic for late-season hunters, but it applies mainly to the beginning of the post-rut period when bucks are moving less in daylight hours. Its effectiveness only lasts a few days, or perhaps a week or two, yet as this period progresses, many things happen that will make it more possible for you to beat the odds and kill a mature buck. ■

19
Second Rut Madness

The final rut of the year is usually called the "second rut" by avid hunters who fight it to the bitter end. Some consider it the best and last opportunity to shoot a mature buck. One thing I'm sure of: Sometimes the second rut is the time to kill a whopper and some tactics are more reliable than others for taking that late-season trophy.

You see, the second rut needs a little explaining, since many folks have the wrong idea about this part of the breeding cycle. There are lots of factors that might contribute more to your chances of taking a big whitetail buck during the post-rut period than the second rut itself. Don't get me wrong. The second rut provides a great opportunity if you fully understand the mechanics of it, have the time to hunt,

Only a small percentage of yearling does come into estrous their first year. When they do, it's usually several weeks after the mature does have bred.

and then get the right breaks. However, other things happen during the winter that can really boost your odds of taking a trophy buck in late season, such as the whitetail's hunger pains. His need for adequate nutrition must be satisfied.

First, you should know that mature does have little or no bearing on the second rut. Nope! Most of them—those one and one-half-years and older—will come into estrous during the first rut, and they will breed and impregnate at that time.

Lots of hunters think the does that didn't get bred during the first rut decide when the second rut will arrive. That is partially correct. Does that don't impregnate during the first rut will come into estrous again about thirty days later. But let's be practical. Do you really think for a moment that a doe is going to walk around in estrous, ready to breed for more than twenty-four hours, and end up getting the cold shoulder from every buck she encounters? You and I both know that there are bucks willing to die for a piece of the action. For this reason, we can safely assume that mature does have little or no bearing on the arrival of the second rut.

It is possible that a mature doe will not impregnate during the first breeding cycle, but this is a rare phenomenon. Earlier in this book, I told you about Julie, the old penned deer that continues to breed each year for a few months, yet never impregnates. There are other tales, and we can all appreciate having such does in our area during the late season.

However, there's another side to the story worth hearing. While writing this

A mature doe will come into estrous about thirty days after the first estrous cycle. However, this is rare since most mature does will breed and impregnate during the first rut.

book, Kelsey, a five-year-old captive doe, impregnated in November during the first rut when she came into estrous. On June 2, the healthy doe delivered three fawns. I arrived on the scene late and watched the last two being born. Kelsey responded to the fawns, cleaned them up and fed them faithfully for the next twenty-four hours. Then all Haiti broke loose.

Thirty-six hours after Kelsey gave birth, I saw the old buck in the four-acre pen sniffing her south end. Moments later, he climbed on her back and did what none of us can believe. The buck's growing antlers were in velvet and the temperature was in the high eighties. But that didn't matter to the buck. He continued to breed Kelsey for the next thirty-two hours, which proves that bucks are always willing. Meanwhile, the old doe did not give her youngsters the time of day. They were desperate to feed, and displayed their emotions by walking around bleating the whole time Kelsey was with the buck. Once the breeding ended, the doe would run away from the buck each time he came near. Thankfully, she got back into the fawn-rearing business before it was too late.

Who knows what happened with this doe. Maybe something went haywire with her hormones. Could it happen in the wild? Probably; anything like this is possible. Perhaps that is why I was inclined to believe one individual who claimed he saw a small, spotted fawn in February.

Who knows when the second rut will arrive. Hunt as often as you can, dress for the weather, and you might be out there at the right time. *Photo by Vikki L. Trout.*

Enough said about mature does. It is the yearlings—those that have not yet enjoyed their first birthdays—that will decide when and if you enjoy success during the second rut.

I don't know of any research that provides us with an "average" number of young does that come into estrous their first year. Still, although you should understand that very few six-month-old does come into estrous, you can bet that some will. Being around captive deer for many years, I can attest to only about twenty percent of the yearling does breeding their first year. That one in five, however, can be your ticket to tagging a whopper buck.

The problem is knowing when the hot second rut will occur. Most young does come into estrous about four to six weeks after the primary rut. However, they are not limited to that time period. Moreover, they don't all come into estrous at once. Of the young does that will breed their first year, one might come into estrous three weeks after the primary rut, while another does eight weeks after.

Consider December 31st many years ago when my son and I hunted in southern Indiana. That cold evening we both witnessed three bucks—one of them a wall hanger—chasing one young doe. The primary rut had been over for many weeks, but we witnessed a brief flurry of late-season rut activity, thanks to being in the right place when a young doe came into estrous.

Nevertheless, the second rut is not like your annual New Year's celebration party. It can go unnoticed. You could be sitting in a tree waiting for the fireworks to start, not knowing that the best part is still several weeks away, or worse yet, not knowing that the late-season action has already ended. That's a shame, to say the least, but it's a fact. If you are sitting in the wrong spot when the second rut kicks in, you'll miss the action for sure. You could even miss the action if you are in the right spot. You might also give up too quickly if nothing happens; it's easy to become bored during the late season—unless you experience that one great day that keeps you going back for more.

During the late archery season in Illinois two years ago, I had no idea when or if the second rut would occur. But one cold, fair evening, I spotted a yearling doe heading for a small field. Behind her was a buck. Behind that buck was another

The second rut is never as hot as the first. Unlike the primary rut, it comes without warning and might even go unnoticed.

During the second rut, a hot young doe will promptly bring a mature buck out of hiding.

buck and, well, there were at least two more. Four bucks following one young doe!

I had seen a couple of straggler bucks during the past few days, but both were small. They hadn't been with does, nor had they shown any sign of the second rut. Yet here I was now with four bucks after one doe, and none of them were more than fifty yards from my tree stand.

As the five deer moved into the field, I examined the bucks closely. The first one on the tail of the doe was a mature ten-pointer, which I estimated would score in the high 130s. The next in line was a six-point buck. Another young buck was behind him, followed by what looked like a two-year-old eight-pointer.

After a few minutes, the young doe made a turn toward me. The biggest buck followed and I raised my bow to prepare for a shooting opportunity, but my hopes only lasted about thirty seconds. When the doe hit the thirty-yard mark, she put on the brakes, threw her head up and scented the air. My scent was blowing right to her and I knew it was over. She promptly ran a short distance into the woods, stopped, and looked back. All the bucks went with her, although that none of them, not even the big buck, had any idea what had bugged the doe. The ten-pointer got after her almost immediately, grunting and finally chasing her over a hill and out of sight. The other bucks followed, hoping the big buck would drop dead of a heart attack so they could get in on the action.

I provided the details of this scenario just to give you an idea of how one little hot doe can attract all kinds of attention. A breeding doe in winter will bring big bucks you never knew existed out of the woodwork and into the hunting arena.

It's really hard to say just how much effect the second rut has on bucks. I believe it does fire them up and sometimes spark them to do those things that bucks love to do during the primary rut. New scrapes are sometimes opened, and old scrapes are sometimes hit. However, I don't know of any avid late-season hunters who have depended upon hunting scrapes for success. In fact, I believe that most late-season scrapes are the result of bucks becoming fired up for the brief period that young does are in estrous. I also believe the mature bucks promptly go back to the usual feeding and bedding habits once the does are done. The scrapes are merely temporary scent stations and will do a hunter no good.

I'm often a bit shocked to locate rubs and scrapes during late season, but never totally surprised. Only last season, I found a couple of scrapes that had been reopened along the edge of a small clover field during the first rut, and they stayed active for a couple of weeks. However, after the rutting activity subsided, they remained idle for about four weeks. I discovered they had been pawed furiously during the late season, but this action was brief, to say the least. In fact, had I hunted near and waited on the scrapes to get hit again, it would have taken about nine months—until the primary rut the following year.

The same is probably true for rubs; you probably can't count on them to produce action. There are exceptions, though, such as the rub line I found during the late archery season several years ago, about five weeks after the primary rut.

I seldom locate fresh rubs in the late season, and when I do, I rarely consider setting up an ambush nearby. This time it was different. I had just passed through the area three days earlier and hadn't seen any rubs. So when I discovered about ten to twelve rubs, all within a one hundred-yard stretch connecting to a thicket and probable bedding area, I had to set up a stand.

Nothing showed for two hours on the first morning I hunted the stand. Around 8:00 A.M., though, I spotted movement to the south. I saw gleaming white antlers bobbing up and down with each step the big ten-pointer took. He was walking precisely along the rub line, and I knew that if he stayed on course, he would pass by at twelve yards. He did. My arrow hit a little too far back, but the doomed buck still went down only 150 yards from where I shot him.

I can honestly say that most of my late-season second-rut action has occurred in the afternoons, long before dusk. Don't get me wrong; I've seen bucks at both dawn and dusk during late season if there was a young hot doe in the area. But most second rut activity, such as bucks pursuing young does, takes place early in the afternoons.

The previously mentioned late-season buck has been the only one I've taken along a rub line. Today, I typically don't depend upon rub lines, or scrapes for that matter, for any second-rut success.

Late-season rutting behavior is probably more common among mature bucks (those that do most of the breeding) than we realize. I believe breeding is always on their minds, even when there is no pretty little doe around. I made a disturbance while preparing a ground blind one year in late season, many weeks after the primary rut. I was clearing a couple of shooting lanes when I heard something behind me, turned, and spotted a huge buck standing there. Maybe he thought all the breaking of limbs meant there was a battle going on. But he noticed me at the same moment I noticed him, and that buck was gone in a flash.

If you stop and think about the tactics that lead to success during the second rut, they're really not much different than those you use in the primary rut. You hunt for the does! If you find yearlings coming into estrous, you will find bucks. If there are no breeding does, you wait them out and hope that sooner or later one will breed. That's the good news about the second rut. It only takes one hot little rascal to pull all the bucks out of hiding. From one day to the next, your hunting area can change from "poor to superb."

Finding the does is a pretty straightforward task. You just find out where they are feeding. Sometimes, it's helpful to locate a bedding area, but it's usually foods, particularly anything green, that will lead to late-season action.

20
Head for the Greens

During the post-rut period, I seriously doubt that anything is more important to a mature buck than feeding. So it's true that a late-season hunter will have the best opportunity of shooting a trophy whitetail if he or she hunts near a food source. It beats the heck out of counting on the second rut, or hunting trails and bedding areas.

Of course, success depends upon the availability of food and the hunter's ability to locate the most attractive forage. That means anything green. Green plants are not plentiful, but most areas do have at least a short supply in winter. More about those foods in a moment.

As you know, the early deep-freeze affects the whitetail's food sources immediately, and the situation worsens as winter progresses. It is one reason a hunter should concentrate on food sources to ambush a late-season buck. But there's more good news for hunters. As the hunting pressure recedes, bucks move more freely and often become more consistent, feeding at certain times each day. All geographical areas are different, and so are the effects of winter on them. However, one thing is certain: deer must feed frequently to restore body fat for the remainder of winter, and body heat for day-by-day survival.

In the late season, it's probably more dependable to hunt close to the food sources than to depend upon the second rut.

183

Knowing what a deer will eat is the first step in tagging a late-season buck, but it might be easier to name the things wintering whitetails won't eat. Just because a particular food is not nutritious and loaded with protein doesn't mean a deer won't eat it. I remember one cold winter when deep snow covered the ground for about three weeks. While driving a back road one evening, I came upon a harvested cornfield that had been picked months earlier. Deer had not visited the field in nearly as long, yet that evening I spotted numerous whitetails, including one respectable buck, feeding on the corn stubbles that stuck above the snow. This is probably one of the least nutritious foods in the deer's habitat, but it became the choice at the time because it was available.

You've already read about the whitetail's food sources earlier in this book. Locating food sources is beneficial for hunting big bucks in autumn, since it enables you to pattern them more accurately, and during the post-rut period it is absolutely essential. However, you should know that the autumn foods previously discussed are usually not around in late season, and the nutritional value of most foods drops considerably from autumn to winter. Deer will naturally select those foods with the highest protein content, but sometimes in winter, their top choice is simply starvation food.

The best method for locating the hottest late-season food source is to cover ground. However, keep in mind that trails don't always tell the story. In other words, trails riddled with tracks are not necessarily highways to hot food sources. In winter, when freezing and thawing occurs, trails always look good due to sparse vegetation, and tracks seem to last forever. It's also true that many whitetails travel in larger groups.

Although snow affects the whitetail's winter food supply severely, all foods become scarce in the late season, even if snow is not a factor.

In many areas, the mast is gone by the arrival of the late season. Snow might also force the deer to feed on high browse.

It is common for deer to bunch up in winter, and three or four walking single file will leave lots of sign along a trail. In fact, even if no trail existed before, one will after the deer pass through.

Yarding is not really a factor in this day and age, except in some isolated northern regions. Researchers have noted that deer will often winter in certain areas when the snow reaches a certain depth. It is also believed that they might move to wintering yards when the days shorten.

I pay more attention to droppings than any other sign, since numerous droppings usually tell a more positive story than numerous tracks. If the droppings are concentrated in a small area, you can bet a food source is close.

The nut mast, such as acorns and beechnuts, has usually dissipated by the time winter arrives, or it may be covered in snow. I said "usually," since there are exceptions. One year in late season, I located a stand of black pin oaks near a fence line, with numerous small, bitter acorns all over the ground. The deer sign near them was impressive enough for me to set up a stand without hesitation. I did not see any wall hangers while hunting there in the week that followed, but I did see numerous whitetails and a few small bucks. I might add, my son John did cash in on a fat doe near the pin oaks just before the season ended. This location was truly a hot winter food source.

If whitetails' movements are limited by snow, you can bet their food sources are extremely limited, too. The less distance they can travel, the less chance they will find food. Deer will browse on the twigs they can reach, and browse lines are common in areas where snow remains on the ground for extended periods. This food source all too often runs out quickly, however.

Some hunters in the Northeast claim that late-season hunting is best near apples. If there are abundant frozen apples on the ground, deer will dig them out, even if they're covered in deep snow. I've seen the same thing happen with persimmons, which usually ripen in October and become an early-season favorite. In one area of the Midwest, I found a clump of five persimmons (all growing out of the same trunk) that had hundreds of the fruits still hanging during the cold days of January, a couple of weeks before the late archery season closed. Although the snow was about six inches deep, there was hardly any under the trees. I saw droppings and tracks everywhere. Unfortunately, I couldn't hunt on top of the persimmons because they were located in a grown-up field, so I set up stands for my wife and I in a nearby woodlot. My wife spotted two groups of bucks, and a few of them were wall hangers, but they never came into bow range. Still, since discovering the persimmons, we now make it a point to check them out each late season.

Earlier I mentioned that deer prefer foods high in protein, but that's not always true. White cedar is never at the top of the deer's food chain, except in winter. It is low in protein, but when there is little else to choose from, it is usually more easily reached than other starvation foods, even those that offer more protein. Aspen, for example, is richer in protein, but deer prefer white cedar, which is more easily digested.

Biologists consider red cedar true starvation food, because it is not as nutritious as white cedar. Deer eat it when they have to, but they could starve to death even when red cedar is available, unless they get a little something else to supplement their diet. Red cedar alone might not get them through the winter.

Winter whitetails will nibble on bramble bushes, such as raspberry and blackberry, if they are available. Seldom do the leaves remain on the vines, but the vines themselves are edible. Again, these are not highly nutritious foods, but during winter nutrition is not always an option.

There are high-protein green foods in some areas, however, and if you have them, the stage is set for you to enjoy late-season hunting at its finest. Green foods are often limited, but the less of them you have, the easier it is for you to narrow down the best areas for ambushing a late-season trophy.

Clover and alfalfa may or may not become staple winter foods. Weather is a factor. I often hunt near these fields in autumn and I have seen my share of bucks near them, when they are located in the right areas. Unfortunately, an extended deep freeze will often annihilate these green fields, and deer will stop using them immediately once this occurs.

That happened to me a couple of years ago. I maintained a clover field all

If available near cover, winter wheat will attract deer consistently in the late season. The wheat will remain an active food source until snow covers the field. *Photo by Vikki L. Trout.*

summer. It was prime and thick when autumn arrived, and several deer utilized the field. Nevertheless, an early-season cold front, which dumped heavy frosts each night, flattened my clover. The fresh deer sign disappeared and the sightings abruptly stopped.

Winter wheat is by far the best late-season crop. Many fields will have new green shoots after a warm autumn, but winter wheat is like a magnet, attracting whitetails in considerable numbers. Of course, the less they have to choose from, the more the deer prefer the wheat. Moreover, you can also assume that the worse the weather, the better the wheat. Wheat, however, is affected by deep snow if it has not grown taller than the snow's depth, which is often the case with late-season snow.

It's a different story when it comes to honeysuckle, however. When I hunted the late firearm season last year, the primary rut had ended about two weeks earlier. The wheat, about two inches tall, had been attracting deer each evening, and on one occasion, I spotted a good buck skirting the edge of the field. Unfortunately, I failed to shoot him before he reached cover, but I remained hopeful that I would see the buck again. Snow fell and covered the field, and the deer deserted it immediately, so I decided to check out a nearby honeysuckle thicket smack-dab in the middle of woodlot.

That small plot of honeysuckle was riddled with tracks and droppings. It looked so good, I didn't waste any time setting up a portable stand within fifteen yards of the thicket.

Later that day, thirty minutes after I climbed into my stand, a few does and fawns came in to feed on the honeysuckle for a few minutes. Moments after they left, I spotted movement to the north: antlers against the snowy background. It was the same buck I had seen by the winter wheat. In less than a heartbeat, the slug zipped through the buck's vitals. The nine-pointer ran only forty yards before piling up in the nearby honeysuckle thicket.

Bear in mind, this particular pocket of foliage was no more than fifty yards around. There was downed timber, which made it idea for honeysuckle to sprout, and although there are other thickets in the area, this particular patch happened to be located in a prime spot. It had timber on three sides and the winter wheat field where I first hunted on the fourth.

I've experienced other successes in and near honeysuckle, but this buck was one of the best I ever took while hunting this late-season food source. It also happened quickly. You can bet that I will be back there for more action next winter, if I still carry a tag.

Harsh winter elements have little effect on honeysuckle. The leaves remain green all year, and they stay on the vine. Several days of bitter cold temperatures

The author shot this buck in late season after setting up a portable stand near a thick patch of honeysuckle. Honeysuckle remains green year-round and is considered a favorable food source in winter. *Photo by Vikki L. Trout.*

do make them brittle, so they fall easily, but there are always plenty of leaves available for whitetails.

Although honeysuckle thrives in many areas, it is not native to North America. You can bet that it's here to stay, and that next winter a few hunters will enjoy success near this lush greenery.

Unfortunately, late-season foods often change from one season to the next, so that any given one might or might not be available. It's also true that weather may have more effect on the food source from one year to the next. A hunter has to stay on top of the food sources if he or she hopes to cash in on a wintertime trophy.

Winter browsing will impact the growth of plants in the upcoming spring. Browsing is not as stressful on plants when they are dormant, but heavy browsing may cause some greens to die. Nevertheless, despite her occasionally vicious attitude, Mother Nature works in mysterious ways. Some plants actually respond positively to winter browsing.

A fresh bed not far from a honeysuckle patch. The deer probably chewed its cud here while resting. *Photo by Fiduccia Enterprises.*

Although your chances of tagging a big buck are better if you know the foods, we also know that Old Man Winter controls the situation. The elements seriously affect when the whitetail will move and feed, and they will often determine how and when you can hunt. ▪

21
The Mid-Day Advantage

The title of this chapter should shed some light on its contents. You're thinking that I'm going to tell you that your best chance of shooting a big buck during post-rut is in the middle of the day.

Sometimes in winter, the best hunting will occur during midday. Sometimes, though, the best hunting is early morning and late evening, just like the good old days. It's really a matter of understanding the late season, the effects of weather, and how deer move differently in various geographical areas.

I've said before that post-rut bucks are similar to pre-rut bucks in that they are more creatures of habit than they are during the primary rut. However, in winter it only takes a little change in weather or food sources to blow that theory right out of the woodlot.

Snow provides an excellent opportunity to find out where deer are going and where they came from. However, for the most reliable sign, you should begin scouting twelve to twenty-four hours after a fresh snowfall.

Consider my late-season archery hunt a couple of years ago. Temperatures had been bitter for several days, and although my wife, Vikki, and I desperately wanted to climb into tree stands early, our better judgment prevailed. Thus, we put off our hunt until 9:30 A.M. It was still rough. The temperature hovered around fifteen degrees when we climbed the tree, but that was a little better than the single-digit the thermometer had shown at 6:00 A.M., when dawn was breaking.

After a couple of hours of boredom, I finally heard the familiar sound of deer approaching. I spotted no less than seven whitetails walking in single file, using a trail about fifty yards from my stand. I examined each closely, but none carried headgear.

Seeing the deer kept me in the stand for a little longer, and that almost led to a big pay-off. Twenty minutes after the does and fawns passed through, I heard another deer approaching—a respectable buck that was probably around 125 inches. Certainly a qualifier, if he stayed on course. He didn't. Just before crossing the imaginary line that would place him in bow range, he picked up the trail of the does and fawns and followed them. You could call it bad luck, but it wasn't all bad. Just being there at mid-day enabled me to see several deer up and moving, including one buck that could have, with a little luck, become an easy target. That's providing they had stayed on course and the bitter-cold temperatures hadn't affected my ability to draw my bowstring and shoot.

I told this story because it happened recently, and because it provided the perfect example of how effective a midday hunt can be. However, I don't go into the late season planning to hunt during mid day, and don't think for a moment that you should hunt only during mid-day hours during the post-rut period. I go in with the traditional spirit of being there and ambushing a buck in early morning and late afternoon, but prepared to hunt during mid-day when necessary.

THE ONSET OF COLD FRONTS

Previously in this book, I discussed approaching cold fronts and rising barometers, and why they spark bucks to move. To summarize what was said, cold fronts seem to make bucks think about breeding does, triggering a rise in a their testosterone levels. That's good for any hunter waiting on a buck to show up.

The post-rut period is no different than any other portion of the hunting season when it comes to cold fronts. Even if a buck has not pursued a doe in many weeks, or months, he'll probably be on the prowl when the cold front hits. The key for the trophy hunter is to be out there as the front approaches. Bucks move best at the onset of a rising barometer, which usually occurs as the cold air first bumps into the warm air.

Unlike many cold fronts during the pre-rut and primary rut, which come in slowly and may take hours and or even days to arrive, winter fronts often come

An approaching cold front can cause a buck to move at any hour of the day, just as he might have done when the does were breeding.

in fast. They can approach and settle on the area in a few short hours, which means deer could be moving at any time of the day to feed. Keep in mind, also, that hunting pressure has usually subsided and the deer will have calmed down. They don't have a problem visiting an open field or some other visible food source with the sun overhead. So be prepared to jump on a cold front.

Of course, precipitation is quite common with the arrival of a cold front, and during the post-rut, the precipitation is often snow. That could spoil future hunting opportunities, or open a new window of opportunity.

ADVANTAGEOUS SNOW

Snowfall is a great scouting opportunity is in the making. Snow reveals all—where the deer are going and where they came from. I can't tell you how many times I have relied on snow to put me onto the deer in winter. I just locate and follow tracks to bedding areas and the hottest food sources.

To get the most out of scouting in snow, consider the best time to do it. I prefer to begin scouting twelve to twenty-four hours after the snow falls. I positively don't want to wait longer. The most productive sign is that which is left within a day of accumulation. After snow has been on the ground two or three days, you can count on finding tracks almost everywhere.

Woody Williams used the snow to his advantage during late season a few years

Indiana bowhunter Woody Williams took this late-season trophy after locating fresh sign in the snow.

ago. New snow had fallen the previous day. Woody arrived early in the afternoon and covered plenty of ground, checking several trails that crossed roads before setting up a stand in a thick grove of pines. Obvious tracks led him to believe that the deer were using the area, and sure enough, a huge ten-pointer appeared shortly before dusk. I helped Woody drag the fine late-season buck out of the pines about one hour later.

Avoid walking and scouting if noise is an issue. Snow usually allows you to move about quietly, but sometimes bitter cold temperatures freeze the top inch of snow. The longer you put off scouting, the more likely you will have to plow through the snow and create a disturbance. Nevertheless, there are advantages to snow being on the ground for long periods.

In chapter 20, I discussed an Illinois buck I harvested last year. A few inches

The longer snow is on the ground, the better the chance that deer will move during mid-day hours. As the sun melts some of the crusting snow, food is often exposed.

of snow had been on the ground for several days. You might also remember me saying that I had first hunted near a winter wheat field that had been a hot food source before the snow. When this snow-covered field, like others in the area, became a deserted arena, I headed for a more promising area, a honeysuckle thicket not far from the winter wheat field.

During the pre-rut period, I attempt to pattern bucks, knowing good and well my best chance of ambushing a trophy depends upon understanding his habits. When the rut is in high-gear, I'm usually hunting hot scrape lines or those areas where does will attract bucks. In a very cold winter, particularly when snow prevails, it's a completely different ball game. Keep in mind, the longer snow is on the ground, the more difficult it is for deer to find food. Thus in winter, when food is an issue, I view hunting bucks and does the same way, and I stick with two tried-and-true methods: I hunt the limited food sources or the bedding areas. When there's snow, the food sources are usually my top choice.

The arrival of snow is seldom productive for hunting. Deer will usually remain bedded or stand around in the densest vegetation. Hunting during a snowfall, particularly a light, dry snow, is enjoyable; you can't beat the scenery. Nonetheless, you're much better off hunting after the snow ends. That's when most deer will get up and move, anxious to feed within a couple of hours. If temperatures are cooperative, they will sometimes move within minutes of the snow ending.

Hunting during a snowfall is seldom productive. Shortly after the snow ends, however, can be a whole different story.

DIVING TEMPERATURES

Snow is not always a factor when hunting post-rut bucks. In many areas, there's no snow at all. In most portions of the Midwest, where I pursue whitetails, cold temperatures are a far more major concern than precipitation.

I've read that when temperatures drop into the single digits, it's best to hunt during the warmest part of the day. I agree totally with this tactic, but there are other considerations.

You see, whether or not deer will move at the warmest part of the day depends upon how cold it gets and what deer are used to in any given geographical area. I've had veteran hunters from Minnesota and Wisconsin tell me that when the temperature drops into the single digits at night, they see deer moving most during the warm

Hunt during mid-day when cold temperatures prevail in winter, since deer prefer moving at the warmest part of the day. However, what is cold to the deer in one area might not be cold to those in another area. *Photo by Vikki L. Trout.*

mid-day hours. I've heard others say that daytime movement is most noticeable when the temperature is near zero degrees.

In my neck of the woods, when the temperature is around fifteen degrees, I commonly see deer moving at the warmest part of the day. I think it all boils down to what deer are used to in a given area.

Thus, you can bet that winter deer typically prefer to move during the warmest hours to conserve body heat. But don't think for a moment that all deer are watching the same thermometer.

Something else to consider is a rapid approaching warm front. Cold fronts make conditions right for killing a buck, but if the cold air has prevailed for several days, the arrival of warm air is sure to spark deer movement. They love going on a feeding binge just when snow and ice begin to melt.

ENDURING THE ELEMENTS

You've probably heard it a hundred times before: You have to wear proper clothing to hunt winter bucks. Over the years, I've written a couple of magazine articles about winter clothing, and a few jillion other writers have followed suit.

Therefore, I won't go into the basics of wearing breathable clothing, wool, and other natural fibers that will keep you outdoors longer in cold and miserable weather. I will say, though, that many hunts are cut short because hunters are not prepared.

So I'm going to pass along a few suggestions to help you endure the elements. After all, if you can't stick around long enough for something to happen, you certainly can't take advantage of a post-rut buck's weaknesses.

Cold feet are the primary reason many hunters can't hack the elements. I know, because I'm

A quality pair of boots will be comfortable and keep your feet warm and dry. An added benefit of camouflage and a scent control system will further aid in bagging a trophy buck. *Photo by Georgia Boot.*

a perfect example. Perhaps it is because they were severely frost bitten when I was young, or just because I happen to be one of those people whose feet are hyper sensitive to the cold. What really matters is that I know how to overcome this hindrance.

First, let's set the records straight about pac boots. Lots of catalogs show these boots in their ads, usually with snow and ice in the background. The thousand words these pictures tell lead you to believe that your feet will stay warm in sub-zero temperatures. Then there are those confusing ratings. Don't believe that pac boots with a temperature rating of minus twenty to zero degrees will keep your feet toasty when the thermometer plunges to ten degrees below zero. Nope! Pac boots might help your feet stay warmer a little longer than your leather boots, but that does not mean they will let you stay on stand for hours. Even in some of the best quality pac boots, I've found additional help might be necessary.

Moisture is the main cause of cold feet. The farther you walk getting to a stand, the more your feet sweat, and once feet get wet, your warm minutes are numbered. The wrong kind of boots might also make your feet sweat, as do boots that are too tight.

Wearing larger boots than normal with one or more pairs of socks is better than wearing boots that fit snug. It's not usually feasible to change socks and boots once you get where you're going. Who wants to carry in extra footwear and change when the air is sharp enough to freeze skin on contact? Fortunately, there are foot warmers, nifty little pouches that work. Moreover, they provide warmth for hours, even when you have damp feet.

Try packing in a pair of boot blankets. They are a little cumbersome to put on and stand in after climbing into a tree stand, but they do keep body heat in and cold air out. I often use them when hunting on the ground, and have found them unbeat-able. Just make sure you get extra large so you can wear your regular boots and slip them into the boot blankets easily.

Finally, consider your style of hunting hat. The baseball cap looks stylish and might match your camo suit perfectly, but it doesn't do a great job of keeping body heat from escaping your head. If I do wear a baseball cap, I make certain to put on a heavy facemask after arriving on stand. I prefer to wear a heavy fabric sock hat, and occa-sionally I wear the older style Jone's cap. Both provide plenty of insulation, although they might affect your hearing ability.

In addition to keeping your feet warm, keeping your head and ears warm with a quality hat like this wool cap made by C.C. Filson allows you to remain on stand longer. Remaining on stand longer gives you greater opportunities to see and bag a dream buck. *Photo by Fiduccia Enterprises.*

No matter what you hunt, hearing is important—sometimes vital to success. Just knowing an animal is there before you see it is often the only chance you have to get prepared. However, in winter it's often wiser to sacrifice hearing for warmth.

I will readily admit that there are probably more reasons not to hunt than there are reasons to hunt during the cold days of winter. After all, there are fewer deer left once the rut is over, hunting pressure has turned others into woodland ghosts, and then there are Mother Nature's raw handouts to deal with. However, I look at it this way: It's the last chance to cash in on a wall-hanger for another season. Despite the old saying, "It ain't over till it's over," when the hunting season ends in winter, by golly it is over. And yet even when it ends, there is a little something left that you can do to boost your potential for success in the upcoming season. ■

22
Beat the Post-Season Blues

I f you feel discouraged, knowing the deer hunting has ended for another season, consider post-season scouting. The idea is nothing new to most hunters, but you might be surprised to hear about some of the methods that can effectively increase your chances of tagging a trophy whitetail when the season rolls around again.

I remember one of my earliest experiences. It was late February and I had walked through a wooded area, scouting for the upcoming spring turkey season. Although I was looking for turkey scratchings and prime roosting areas, I stumbled upon something else that was equally intriguing. A large scrape, perhaps five feet across, on the border between a dense thicket and the hardwoods. No doubt the bucks had worked on it consistently during the hunting season that had ended more than sixty days earlier. I stood gazing at the scrape for the next few minutes, making a vow to return the following deer season.

The primary rut was still three weeks away when I came back in October, but the bucks had already opened the scrape. In fact, I wasted no time setting up a tree stand about sixty yards from it. I would have gotten closer had a large tree been there to hold

my stand; instead, I had to settle for a small black oak that provided just enough foliage to keep me hidden. In the weeks that followed, I hunted as often as the wind direction allowed. I saw no less than six different bucks visit the scrape, including one wall hanger. That bigger buck did not pass by close enough to offer a shooting opportunity, but I did discover one important fact: Post-season scouting *does* pave the way for future opportunities. Whether you locate deserted scrapes, abandoned rub lines (my personal favorite), or a large shed antler (on second thought, *that's* my favorite), it gives you a starting point for next year.

The author took this respectable eight-pointer near a traditional rub line. He located the rub line while post-season scouting months earlier. *Photo by Vikki L. Trout.*

With the passing of another hunting season, it is easy to understand why many hunters believe the big bucks now rest on a trophy wall or in the freezer. After all, if you hunt consistently throughout the season, you have experienced both the best and the worst: A few bucks in the rut, then the boring days of the late season. More than likely, you saw the firearm season take its toll on what few trophy bucks roamed your favorite stomping grounds. Statistics show that the bulk of the harvest during the firearm season consists of bucks under two years old, and in some states, the harvest of yearling bucks often surpasses eighty percent of the total buck harvest. Even when I find old buck sign during post-season, I always wonder if the buck that visited the scrape, or made the rub, is alive or dead.

Thankfully, there are always survivors. Some yearling and mature bucks do escape, and we can assume a trophy buck or two will roam our area next season. Even better, though, is the sign left behind by those survivors. If a hunter can locate this sign before the spring growth cycle begins, he or she may find where the bucks will soon be. Let's not forget, whitetails are creatures of habit (trophy bucks are no exception), often relying on the same food sources, bedding areas, and rub and scrape lines year after year.

WITHERED RUBS AND SCRAPES

By the time your post-season scouting begins, you can be thankful there is little or no foliage with which to contend. Barren woods make it possible for us to spot scrapes and rubs that were left behind long ago.

So what good does it do for the hunter to locate old rubs and scrapes? First, consider that many rub and scrape lines become consistent travel routes for bucks every season. You may also discover a hideout or bedding area after following these old, but travel-marked trails.

Following old rubs and scrapes during post-season may lead you to buck hideouts. Many bucks choose the same dense bedding areas every year during the pre-rut period.

Finding post-season rubs and scrapes is not difficult if you are willing to cover ground. However, the location of these old markers has a lot to do with the action you are likely to find the following hunting season. For instance, finding a rub or scrape here or there does not necessarily mean you can count on a buck showing up in the same location the next year. A buck might rub several trees and make many scrapes over a large area when in rut. Some of these markers have little or no bearing on his regular travel routes, so you must think wisely when looking for this valuable sign.

In farm country, I do not spend my time searching for scrapes and rubs along the edges of agricultural fields. They are usually territory or coincidental markers. However, I do walk funnels, fencelines, and woodlots that provide cover. Not all of these areas will have an abundance of scrapes and rubs, but I can count on finding a distinctive rub or scrape line every now and then. Once I find them, I can rest assured a few bucks traveled the route during the rut, or even better, the pre-rut.

I also make it a point to look for rubs made during the rut in previous years. Many of these may be more difficult to see, since they are blackened on the tree from weather and aging, but they do provide proof that bucks used the travel route for several years.

I remember one farmland area where I discovered several old rubs. Many were two or three years old, but could still be seen within a few feet of a new rub. No doubt, there had been several rub lines here before. Some of the trees with old rubs were also dead (this is why I always look closely at dead trees, particularly cedars and pines). It also seemed likely that a

Not all old rubs will show you where the bucks will be. However, old rub lines that seem to follow the same trails year after year may lead you to good ambush locations.

hunter could count on the rub line to bring in a buck or two during the hot portion of the pre-rut. I hunted near the rub line on two occasions and saw no less than three different bucks. I would have seen more, no doubt, had it not been for one eight-pointer that fell victim to my Muzzy broadhead shortly after daylight.

I *do* focus on large scrapes, since they may become active primary scrapes every year near the end of the pre-rut period. One example was the scrape mentioned at the beginning of this chapter. However, a scrape line found after the hunting season is often your best bet the next fall.

Scrapes may be harder to see than rubs because of leaves or debris that cover them. When walking the funnels and fencelines in farm country, they usually can be spotted because there may be fewer leaves to cover them. When in dense wooded areas, though, I like to walk deer trails that adjoin master trails. Bucks often use secondary trails as they travel to master trails. It also helps to examine the limbs hanging above the leaf-covered scrapes, since chewed limbs confirm the seriousness of the scrape.

UNDISCLOSED HIDEOUTS

We can see how an old rub or scrape line can help you locate a promising ambush area for next year's rut. However, finding a post-season rub and scrape line might also provide opportunities for the pre-rut season, before the bucks have started thinking about breeding.

In the early fall, you can count on most bucks sticking to certain bedding areas. The bucks may travel different routes to reach these bedding areas, but they are somewhat consistent when it comes to lying up in the same vicinity each day. They like places where they are left alone, and where cover gives them the necessary sense of security. These bedding areas may last for only a short time, depending on the harvesting of crops and the thinning of foliage. However, you can get the jump on these hideouts by locating post-season rub and scrape lines.

I love to follow the scrapes and rubs I find after the hunting season ends, because they can lead me to a buck's bedding area. True, the buck that used the hideout may no longer be in this world, but you often can count on another taking up residence there.

The distance needed to follow the old rub and scrape lines may vary, but you can safely assume that the buck did not travel far during the early season, when temperatures were warm. Once I follow the route to a dense area, such as a stand of pines, a cutover area or a thicket, I usually assume I have found a bedding area that once attracted a buck, and might do so again the next autumn. New rubs and scrapes may not show up for quite some time, but I can at least believe that a buck is using the same trail that led me to the bedding area.

SHED ANTLERS

They say that seeing is believing, and I must agree. There is nothing I like better than knowing a big buck exists in an area where I intend to hunt. But the only way to know for sure is to see the buck after the hunting season ends, before he sheds his antlers—or to find those sheds.

Since I am an avid spring turkey hunter, I usually find myself in the field during the late winter and early spring, scouting for gobblers. I often focus my attention on the ground, looking for turkey scratchings, droppings, and feathers. Sheds can be spotted easily at this time of year, before squirrels, mice, and other critters have had the chance to consume them for their calcium. I enjoy finding any shed and have a box full of them in my garage. But I especially like find-

Deer hunters who pursue spring turkeys have a great opportunity to locate old rubs, scrapes, and even shed antlers that could put them onto a big bick the next autumn.

ing the big ones, simply because I know that this buck will probably be around during the pre-rut of the upcoming season.

Many agricultural fields where deer congregate during the late winter months are good places to begin shed hunting. Deer may be attracted to these areas simply because they are the only available food source, and you can count on them to spend much of their time in the fields. On one occasion, I located a respectable shed without even leaving my vehicle, thanks to a quality binocular that let me cover the field.

I also walk deer trails, but when I am in wooded areas, I usually find sheds at random, lying about anywhere. In fact, if it were not for my turkey scouting, I would seldom find sheds in dense areas.

I love the challenge of locating both sheds of a buck. It usually doesn't happen, but it's sure fun looking for the second once you find the first. On a couple of occasions, I've found both within spitting distance. Just a couple of months before writing this chapter, I found one antler and my wife found the other. The eight-pointer dropped them about four feet apart.

A large shed is proof there's a big buck in the area. But keep in mind, even the shed of a yearling buck tells you he will be around the following season, carrying a little more headgear. If you find the shed of a probable two-year-old buck, it means that a trophy-class deer will offer you a challenge

Shed antlers provide positive proof of a buck's existence in the area. Keep in mind, the buck that lost the antlers will grow even bigger ones for the next hunting season.

the next fall. As for finding the antler of a three-year-old, we don't even need to go there. You already know how that will get the old heart pumping.

Don't count on finding your best hunting opportunity where you found the sheds. The location of a shed antler in the late winter and early spring has little to do with where the buck will be when the hunting begins. This is particularly true if you find the antler near a food source, since food sources are strictly seasonal. It does, however, let you know that this buck roams your hunting territory. In late season when you locate a shed antler, the buck that dropped it was probably in his home range—not a mile or more away chasing does like he might have been months before shedding. That's a plus for you. Then, when you begin hunting in the pre-rut season, you know the buck is somewhere nearby—anywhere from one hundred yards to one-half mile away. However, you can bet he's probably no farther than that.

Post-season scouting is not necessarily popular amongst most hunters, simply because it does not provide instant results. Most folks want to find sign and see it pay off within days or sometimes hours. I'm a lot like that, too. However, post-season scouting *does* give you an opportunity to be in the field, and allows you to plan for your upcoming hunt with more confidence.

I consider post-season scouting to be just another piece of that complex puzzle we call big-buck hunting. It's that little something extra you can do to beat the odds. Surprisingly, though, there are still more ways you can increase your chances of tagging a mature buck in the season ahead. ■

23
Next Year's Rut

Once the hunting season closes, it's time to start managing your area for next year's rut. Surprisingly, there's a whole lot you can do to maintain a quality deer herd and increase trophy-hunting potential.

First, let me say that owning and leasing land is not necessarily a requirement for properly managing whitetails, but it certainly helps if you own the land, simply because you make the decisions. If you lease land, you need to be in touch with the landowner, who can quickly authorize you to do what is necessary to improve the hunting. But even if you don't own or lease land, there are things you as a hunter can do to contribute to next year's rut, and increase your trophy-hunting potential.

It might mean getting to know a landowner better, and coming up with a sales pitch to convince him to help, or allow you to do the job. Convincing a landowner might seem like a major project , but it's only kernels of corn compared to the harvest you can reap.

SHOOTING ONLY BIG BUCKS

I started deer hunting in the early 1960s, and began pursuing mature bucks about fifteen years ago. Even before I seriously began passing small deer, there was always the hope that a huge buck would appear. Even now, as I write about monster whitetails, I feel a rush come over . . . an inexplicable reaction whenever I think about antlers.

Trophy hunting has been seriously ridiculed by many individuals, including some manufacturers of the outdoor trade. They claim that focusing only on big bucks is damaging to the sport, and does not help young hunters get started. I agree, but there is a very positive aspect to trophy hunting. Consider its economic impact alone! It demands innovative thinking, which has led to the development of numerous useful products. Then there is the challenge: The indisputable fact that trophy hunting has added a whole new exciting dimension to time spent outdoors.

We certainly cannot forget that youngsters are the future of all hunting, and the rigors of trophy hunting should not be pushed on them, or even other hunters who don't pursue big bucks exclusively. Trophy hunting is a personal choice . . . a decision that should always be left up to the individual.

Should hunters pass small bucks in small areas? What good will it do if you don't shoot a buck on the fifty acres where you can hunt? In other words, won't someone else come along and shoot the deer off the property you are managing?

No doubt the buck you pass up might end up field dressed by someone else minutes after it walks by. I've seen it happen. But keep in mind that most of us will never control enough ground to decide which deer will be shot. That happens only in huge tracts consisting of thousands of acres or on high-fence properties. We won't even talk about fenced-hunting operations. If you have read this book, you already know how I feel about them.

No matter how many small bucks you pass up, don't think for one minute that all of them will end up dead. It won't happen. Yes, you will increase harvest opportunities for others, but even they will fill tags and move on. Here's one way to look at it: If you pass up six subordinate antlered bucks, of which five are hammered before the season ends, there's still one buck that could reach trophy potential.

Don't bother dreaming about areas that have lots of big bucks. If such places exist, I've never been fortunate enough to find one. Some areas are consistently better than others, and that's exactly why I choose to hunt them. However, outside of deer pens, I know of no areas where you can count on huge bucks walking by every hour. There are outstanding properties other than fenced operations, where you can pay out big money and have a good chance at seeing a super buck, but then again, this book has been focused on advanced hunting strategies for the lands most of us hunt close to home.

MANAGING THE BUCK-TO-DOE RATIO

Should you shoot does and will this practice increase your chances of shooting a wall hanger? The answer is "absolutely" on both counts. Having too many does around is bad business for your hunting area.

Previously in this book, I discussed one place where EHD hit hard. We discovered numerous dead deer, mostly does, in a square mile area. The whitetail population was drastically reduced in this Indiana county, but the bucks went crazy during the rut. They moved consistently, knowing they had to if they were to find a breeding doe.

That's just one example of how fewer does increased buck sightings. States and provinces manage deer herds by increasing the legal number of does that can be harvested. They do it to control the deer populations, not to increase your trophy hunting potential. It's usually effective, but I've seen some of these management practices cause serious side effects. We still need a substantial deer herd. More deer usually means more hunting opportunities, more youngsters getting involved, and more veteran hunters continuing to buy licenses every season.

Although some states and provinces have enacted depredation programs to control increasing deer herds, some folks don't believe in a few of the rules governing this management practice. For instance, Indiana allows deer to be shot with high-powered rifles beginning in late June in some areas. Please note: Hunters are restricted to using slugsters and blackpowder guns during the actual deer season. In addition, when a doe is depredated in June or July, it could reduce the herd by three. Consider that the future is never bright for unweaned fawns. Bucks are also shot, which doesn't do

Shooting does could help you maintain a better buck-to-doe ratio and increase trophy trophy-hunting opportunities.

anything much for hunters who could have tagged that buck in the upcoming season.

There are ways to control doe populations and increase your buck-to-doe ratio during the hunting season. Even if you don't want to shoot does, you can have someone else do it for you, such as youngsters or other hunters who want the meat. Alternatively, you can consider shooting does and donating the meat to needy folks, or to a landowner who has been kind enough to let you hunt.

One word of warning: If you choose to shoot a doe, do so at the right times. By that, I mean you don't want to shoot a doe when there is a darned good chance a buck will be following her. Nor do you want to shoot a doe in an area where you have patterned a huge buck. Killing does can screw up a hunting area more than you might realize. Wait until late in the season, or after harvesting your big buck.

It's never easy determining how many does there are to each buck, but hunters who are in the field consistently probably know better than some biologists. In fact, some of us hunters think of ourselves as unofficial wildlife managers. Let's assume that you determine how many does there are by the number you see. Make sure you do not count deer after the firearm season, when many bucks have already bit the big one.

One thing we do know is that we *don't* always know how many does to shoot in a given area. Some places can sustain bigger reductions than others. Habitat—food and cover—is the key. The right diversity, say sixty percent food and forty percent cover, or vice versa, might permit the killing of thirty percent of the does each year. On the other hand, mountainous areas, big timber and some other kinds of terrain experience a drastic decline in its deer population for years to come if a thirty percent harvest of does occurred.

Areas with five or more does to each buck probably will not offer quality trophy hunting. There are other factors to consider, but in most cases, two or three does to each buck is better. That means you will have more trophy hunting potential, see more buck sign, and you might even enjoy a longer rut to hunt.

Bedding Areas

You already know what kind of bedding areas appeal to mature bucks. They like it thick. If you have such areas on the property you hunt, you have a better chance of patterning the bucks utilizing the bedding area, and a better chance of seeing them in daylight hours.

I first got the idea of constructing a bedding area after talking with Tim Hillsmeyer. Tim is conservation minded and he often comes up with great managing ideas—one of them

The author constructed a one-acre bedding area to attract deer. New growth provides both cover and food for whitetails. *Photo by Vikki L. Trout.*

being the construction of a bedding area on a particular forty-acre tract where we sometimes hunt in Illinois. I followed his advice for the first time, and took advantage of his assistance, two years ago. What a difference it made.

The property I speak of has a two and one-half-acre field in the middle. The remaining thirty-seven and one-half acres consists of a couple of ponds and hardwoods, and no thickets. To make the bedding area, we chose about one and one-half acres, one hundred yards from the field. The site consisted of dogwoods, ash, and a few gum, hickory, and maple trees primarily. Cutting the trees had opened the area and allowed growth, so that it is now overgrown with wild roses, blackberry bushes, and most importantly, honeysuckle. I shot my first big buck near the thicket last year, but saw others using the bedding area, too.

Let me point out that I've never been crazy about cutting trees. It really bothers me. So I am always very selective about what I cut, knowing that if I do it properly, many species of wildlife will benefit. Which means an increase in whitetail diversity and trophy hunting potential.

I would recommend you never construct large bedding areas, since they are seldom necessary. In the near future, I plan to construct another one-acre bedding site about three hundred yards from the previously mentioned one. Small sites are attractive enough if the right cover surrounds them: possible escape routes with some foliage and trees. A deer will want to leave the bedding area without having to step into the open.

That brings up another point: When making a bedding area, remember to leave openings for deer to walk through. They won't go into areas that are completely surrounded by downed timber, so make certain you cut trees in several locations to allow deer to move about.

I would suggest you not cut mast trees unless absolutely necessary. In the bedding area Tim and I made, we left some oak and persimmon. I did cut some hickories, primarily because of their abundance, and because deer seldom feed on their mast. I did not hurt the squirrel population either, because there were numerous hickory trees outside the bedding area.

You'll be surprised how much food will become available in a newly cut bedding area. Sunlight coming through allows for new growth, which eventually provides a variety of foods. Some will even become favorite late-season choices.

The best time to construct your bedding area is in late winter before the green-up begins, and honeysuckle is probably the best thing to hope for when choosing a site. It provides cover—and great concealment—and a prime food source in winter, when others are no longer available. However, it might be necessary to fertilize your area. Fertilizing need not be an extremely costly endeavor. When accompanied by moisture, it adds necessary ingredients to the soil and speeds the growth process.

ATTRACTIVE FOOD PLOTS

I've also tried my hand at constructing food plots on the same Illinois farm where I built the bedding area. I quickly discovered, though, that food plots might or might not help my trophy-hunting potential. In some areas of the Midwest, you probably won't beat the high-protein and nutritional foods already provided by farmers with big acreage. In other words, the bucks already have what it takes to grow big antlers. Although some regions have an entirely different management practice, food plots in any geographical area can be good for attracting deer.

Be aware, though, that food plots are not the ultimate guarantee for attracting deer, and you shouldn't think of food sources as bait. Sometimes they work—sometimes they don't. What you should consider before taking on the

The most attractive food plots are secluded and more likely to attract a mature buck in daylight hours.

Natural food plots like corn act as magnets to deer. Look for lesser-used trails leading to and from the corn. *Photo by Fiduccia Enterprises.*

responsibility of maintaining a food plot is whether it's necessary, and how much it will cost to do it right.

First, let me say that you don't need major equipment. I sow seed by hand, and I own an old Ford tractor with a disc and bush hog. It's an inexpensive set-up, but it works well for small food plots. I sew seed by hand. Some folks use four-wheelers with attachments to install and maintain food plots.

Maintaining a couple of acres is not really an extremely time-consuming process. Nevertheless, you can always hire someone to do the work if you don't want to buy your own equipment, or don't have the time to invest in working the plot.

You need to know which seeds offer the best potential. I prefer winter wheat,

Food plots, such as this clover field, should be limited to about two acres or less. This will limit the number of locations where deer enter the field, increasing hunting opportunities. *Photo by Vikki L. Trout.*

but whether or not it is wise for you to plant wheat depends upon your location. (Check with your local agricultural office.) Wheat is no problem to maintain, and once autumn foods have vanished, the deer will visit your crop.

Clover and alfalfa are top choices for many people who plant food sources for deer. I like having a red and white clover field of about one and one-half acres and a half acre wheat field. This combination provides food plots for both autumn and winter. Keep in mind, though, the more acorns there are in autumn, the fewer the deer that will be attracted to clover.

There are a large number of seeds to choose from, and many will cost you a bloody fortune. Some will work and some won't. One rule of thumb is competition: Your food plot is most likely to attract deer when their other choices are limited. I know of farms in the south that plant food plots just for attracting deer and enjoy consistent success. However, the same seeds they use don't work in the Midwest, where I reside, because better foods for deer are already here. So the seeds you choose should be matched to your soil and climate.

It's true that when it comes to growing trophy antlers, most nutritional foods come from the best soil. Even if you have the right location for a food plot, you can't grow the high-protein foods all deer want in poor soil. Preferred foods are those that offer a protein level of sixteen percent or more. It takes a little limestone and lots of calcium to grow trophy antlers, and some of the best soils are in bottom lands rich in minerals.

Not many of us have access to such lush terrains, but we can add ingredients to enhance our land's potential for growing and attracting big bucks. First, though, test the pH level of your soil. Your local agricultural office can help. It's easy to take a soil analysis, and not costly. I haven't done this on the property where I construct food plots, but growing trophy antlers isn't my goal. I just want to attract the right customers to the land. A pH level of six or less usually requires additives, such as lime and fertilizer. But not necessarily. It depends upon the crops you intend to grow.

For the best results, keep food plots small, under three acres, and make certain the plot will get sunlight. Those ten acres or more are seldom as dependable. They may provide plenty of food, but they don't increase hunting opportunities as well as small fields. Choosing productive ambush locations is easier when you plant small fields. Narrow forest openings and old road beds are ideal, allowing deer to remain hidden when getting to the food plot, yet feel secure when feeding. Secluded food plots are also more likely to attract deer in daylight hours.

I couldn't see a better way to end this book than with a chapter about managing a deer herd—offering you ways

The soil must have the right pH level to grow certain seeds. If you are in doubt, have an inexpensive soil analysis done to find out what will grow and what you might need to add to improve the soil.

to increase your trophy-hunting opportunities. For the best results, management has to begin in late winter as soon as the hunting ends, and continue through the hunting season for the best results. Although pursuing mature bucks is a never-ending management endeavor, managing food plots, bedding areas and whitetail populations are the easy part of trophy hunting. The most difficult part of tagging a big buck during the three phases of the rut never changes: It is, and always will be, advanced tactics. And, I might add, we're all still learning. ▪

BIBLIOGRAPHY

Alsheimer, Charles. *Hunting Whitetails by the Moon.*
Iola: Krause Publications, 1999.

Alsheimer, Charles. *Quality Deer Management, The Basics and Beyond.*
Iola: Krause Publications, 2002.

Gerlach, Duane; Sally Atwater; and Judith Schnell. *The Wildlife Series: Deer.*
Mechanicsburg: Stackpole Books, 1994.

Rue, Leonard Lee. *The Deer of North America.*
New York, Outdoor Life Books, 1978.

The Wildlife Management Institute. *White-Tailed Deer,
Ecology and Management.*
Mechanicsburg: Stackpole Books, 1984,

WOODS N' WATER
PRESS

Other Outdoorsman's Edge Books available from

Woods N' Water Press

TO ORDER

call us at 1-800-652-7527 or write to us at Woods N' Water Press, P.O. Box 550, Florida, NY 10921
or visit us on the web at www.fiduccia.com or www.outdoorsmansedge.com.